THE ART OF
GAME
CHARACTERS

THE ART OF
GAME
CHARACTERS

LEO HARTAS

ILEX

First published in the United Kingdom in 2005 by

I L E X
3 St Andrews Place
Lewes
East Sussex BN7 1UP

ILEX is an imprint of The Ilex Press Ltd
Visit us on the web at:
www.ilex-press.com

This book was conceived by
ILEX, Cambridge, England

ILEX Editorial, Lewes:
Publisher: Alastair Campbell
Executive Publisher: Sophie Collins
Creative Director: Peter Bridgewater
Managing Editor: Tom Mugridge
Editor: Kylie Johnston
Design Manager: Tony Seddon
Designer: Jonathan Raimes
Junior Designer: Jane Waterhouse

ILEX Research, Cambridge:
Commissioning Editor: Alan Buckingham
Development Art Director: Graham Davis
Technical Art Editor: Nicholas Rowland

British Library Cataloguing-in-Publication Data
A catalogue record for this book is available
from the British Library.

ISBN 1-904705-33-2

Printed and bound in China

For more information on this title please visit:

www.web-linked.com/gachuk

INTRODUCTION

CONTENTS

GAME CHARACTERS

INTRODUCTION

THERE IS A WHOLE NEW POPULACE. SOME ARE TO BEFRIEND, OTHERS TO CONTROL, AND MANY MORE TO FEAR AND FIGHT. STEP INSIDE THE VIRTUAL WORLD, INTO A DIGITAL SKIN, TO BECOME ANYONE YOU WANT.

GAME CHARACTERS ARE RAPIDLY GROWING UP, FROM A HANDFUL OF PIXELS TO FULLY THREE-DIMENSIONAL BEINGS CAPABLE OF LIFE-LIKE MOVES, EVEN LIFE-LIKE THOUGHTS. AS TECHNICAL RESTRICTIONS FALL AWAY, GAME DESIGNERS FIND THEY ARE FREE TO CREATE WHOMEVER THEY IMAGINE, AND, LIKE A DIGITAL FRANKENSTEIN, BRING THEM TO LIFE.

Xiao Qiao from Koei's **Dynasty Warriors 4.**

GAME CHARACTERS WILL BECOME INCREASINGLY IMPORTANT, NOT JUST AS DISTANT DIGITAL ACTORS BUT AS A NEW SOCIAL CIRCLE. AFTER ALL, MANY PLAYERS NOW SPEND MORE TIME WITH THEM THAN WITH THEIR REAL FRIENDS OR FAMILY. THE BEST OF THESE NEW COMPANIONS WILL BE MORE THAN JUST PAINTED POLYGONS; INSTEAD THEY WILL HAVE MOTIVES, EMOTIONS, FEARS, AND DESIRES — PERSONALITIES THAT MAKE YOU CARE.

Above. Lara from **Oni** by Bungie Software.
Opposite. **Prince of Persia: Warrior Within** by Ubisoft.

GAME CUTIES

1

CUTE, BUT NOT NECESSARILY CUDDLY

EVEN GROWN MEN CAN'T RESIST THOSE BIG SAD EYES. CUTE HAS BEEN A BIG PART OF THE GAMES INDUSTRY EVER SINCE THE CUTEST GRANDDADDY OF THEM ALL, PAC-MAN, FIRST APPEARED IN 1980. CUTE CARTOON CHARACTERS WORK WELL IN COMPUTER GAMES FOR THE SAME REASON THAT THEY WORK IN ANIMATED MOVIES AND PRINT CARTOONS: THEY ARE APPEALING AND EXPRESSIVE.

Su Ling from **Legend of Kay** by Neon Studios.

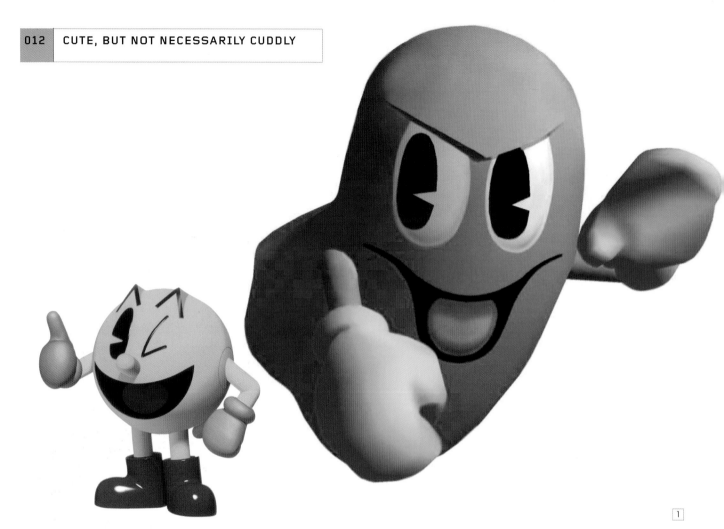

1

Cutesy cartoon characters first appeared around the turn of the twentieth century with Winsor McKay's *Gertie the Dinosaur*, his groundbreaking animation of 1914, and his characters in the *Little Nemo* comic strip. Other characters arrived, such as George Herriman's Krazy Kat, also in 1914, and the wonderful work of James Swinnerton in *Little Jimmy* from 1933. Swinnerton's work is particularly important in that it established the anatomy of cute: a toddler's body proportion with big eyes for all characters, even adults.

A cartoon style was perfect for the technical restrictions of early computer games because it required just a handful of pixels to outline a character, whereas even with today's powerful graphics the quest for realism has yet to be fulfilled. Perhaps the first cute characters to flit across the games screen were the aliens in *Space Invaders*. Although depicted in serried ranks they held a compact, cute charm as they marched down for the kill.

The most famous of all, however, and still an icon of the video game, is *Pac-Man*, designed in 1980 by Namco game designer Moru Iwatani. *Pac-Man* worked because it embodied two great strengths: a brilliantly simple and new game genre, and an instantly recognizable character. Although based on a pizza with a slice missing, its ravenous appetite was amusing, as were the slightly nervous ghosts scurrying after it. Simple as they were, they were characters with character.

1. Pac-Man himself with his adversary, Inky, updated in 3D. Namco.

2–5. The Mario Brothers and friends from Nintendo's **Mario Party 4** and **5.**

1

2

3

4

5

More complex elements of cartoon style were established by Walt Disney when he first drew Mickey Mouse in 1928, while others, such as Roadrunner by Chuck Jones, tested the limits of cartoon distortion. All of these characters have found their way into computer games, but often they have appeared a little diminished, jumping from platform to platform, avoiding tumbling barrels. Perhaps this is because we know them to be more interesting and complex as characters than the restrictions of typical game genres allow.

The most successful comic characters in the digital realm were born in the medium and have gone on to star in an endless succession of games. Sega's Sonic the Hedgehog and Nintendo's Mario Brothers are some of the few game characters to have survived and prospered through a changing series of game consoles. Their success as characters can be partly attributed to their

being designed to do nothing more than bounce around the game's levels at the behest of the player. Only in the most recent iterations have they been called upon to display more depth of character.

These examples highlight an important difference between the animation stars of TV, and those on the end of a joystick: the first is cute and funny and the other is just cute. TV cartoons have the structure of a story and a series of cleverly timed gags to leave the viewer (if the show is any good) doubled up on the sofa with laughter. Games have a completely different structure that typically takes the character, led by the player, through a series of often arbitrary challenges. Gags can be played, such as a Tom-and-Jerry-style flat face whack from an iron, but because the player has to repeat them frequently, they quickly lose any humour they may initially have possessed.

1. Shift's **Bombastic** are characters in a puzzle game. They reflect the very apex of excellent Japanese graphic cute.

2. **Pikmin 2**. Nintendo. No-one can fail to be endeared to these tiny plant characters who are so generous with their help in rebuilding your spaceman character's ship.

Opposite. **Tak 2: The Staff of Dreams** by Avalanche exhibits a cartoon style that could be considered overstated but in its context works well and assures the character is imprinted on the player's mind.

1

1

COMEDY SKETCHING

Graphically the cartoon character has had to undergo quite a change in the move to real-time 3D. Traditionally the characters were 2D, a medium that allowed the artist significant expression of line and cartoon distortion in the animation. Moving to 3D has caused some confusion. For example, when the Flintstones were to receive a 3D makeover the artist had to draw up new turnarounds, because throughout their long history they had never been seen from behind.

It has taken the public time to get used to the idea of sculptured cartoon characters. Some details have been awkward. Eyes, which in 2D were a dot in a flat, white ellipse, had to become

– what? Should it be a 2D texture drawn on the surface of the head, as in *Animal Crossing*? Or protruding 3D balls, which, with the exaggerated cartoon scale of eyeball to head, looks slightly uncomfortable, à la *Mario Bros*?

It took a while to get the lighting and colour right. Early 3D cartoons were lit too naturalistically, so that grey shadows were cast across their smooth, flat-colour chins, making them look like they needed a shave. Later games used coloured, simplified, or cel-shaded shadows and gave the characters a luminance of their own, which against traditionally painted-style backgrounds was as pleasing as traditional animation.

1. **Donkey Kong.**
2–3. **Animal Crossing** by Nintendo is a fascinating computer 'life' toy set, rather than a game. Each character has distinct traits and motivations that the player becomes aware of through interaction.

4. **The Legend of Zelda** by Nintendo. Zelda has seen many different adventures on different consoles, showing how a strong character works whatever the changes in style, fashion, and technology.

5. **Parappa the Rapper** by Sony Entertainment. A wonderful example of two interesting artists, Rodney Alan Greenblat, and the Japanese musician and pop star, Masaya Matsuura, being given free creative rein. The results speak for themselves.

6. Mad cat character from **Monster Hunter,** by Capcom's Production Studio 1.
7. **Starfox Adventures** by Rare and Nintendo. Starfox is furry, but he ain't so cute.

1

2

3

4

5

6

7

8. **Worms** by Team 17 Software has
endured several iterations over a
number of platforms. Here the worm is
seen in its latest 3D incarnation.

8

Very recent cartoon games have begun to experiment with 3D to produce styles that are really at home in the medium. This can be seen in *Animal Crossing,* where a clean, almost childishly simple graphic style in the characters and sets makes them look like paper models. Nintendo's excellent *Legend of Zelda: The Wind Waker* features simply-drawn, outlined characters that look as though they are painted on textured watercolour paper. An older game now, but memorable for its revolutionary style, is artist Rodney Alan Greenblat's work for Sony's *Parappa the Rappa*. Not only are the flat-coloured characters delightful, but the visual play of their cardboard cut-out flatness in a 3D environment is brilliant.

Even without the belly laughs, cuteness works well in computer games because it has a wider market appeal than styles preferred by the 'hardcore' gamer. The lovable characters and varied, often less violent gameplay, attract children, teenage girls, and women while the bright colours and simpler shapes have a vibrancy that perfectly suits the small screen. Of all the characters created in the digital realm it is the cartoon cuties that are most likely to endure and even find the holy grail of all game creators, the bridge to other media.

1. **Sphinx and the Cursed Mummy** by Eurocom. These characters are sculpted with the same assurance and quality as any Pixar star.
2. Captain Olimar and Louie from **Pikmin 2**, by Nintendo.

3. **Rayman** by Ubisoft is a perfect example of a character successfully conceived for the video game. Of note is his lack of limbs – not only a fun visual device, but surely a saving on polygons and animation.

4. Nintendo's benevolent giant, **Doshin**, developed by Param, is an example of original thinking both in game play and character design.

5. **Looney Tunes: Back In Action.** Warner Brothers' classic characters in a game developed by Warthog. The original 2D graphic style finds new life in 3D.

2 3
4 5

INSIDER SECRETS: FUR FIGHTIN'

LEGEND OF KAY

Antony Christoulakis is the lead artist on *Legend of Kay* at Neon Studios in Germany. Young Kay is an apprentice in the martial arts on a mission to save his village from Emperor Shun, king of the gorillas. The game is a classic action adventure.

What are the special requirements of a game character?

'First of all he has to be appealing or charismatic in some sort of way – he doesn't necessarily have to be a beauty to achieve that. He has to fit to the taste and age of your target audience and he should have something human in its nature – something that people know and understand from our real world. If you just design the most weird alien creature you can think of, people will find it hard to create an emotional connection. But he also has to have something new to stand out from the crowd.'

1. Kay in-game.
Opposite. Kay in action. The Meister
(top right), Kay with his uncle, and
facing The Boarax.

Currently, what sort of technical limitations do you have to take into account when designing game characters?

'There are a lot of things to think about during the design phase: limitations in the number of bones, does the engine support cloth simulation to use long or wide cloth, limitations in the number of polygons, et cetera.'

What impact has the increasing sophistication of game engines had on character design?

'I think we have a situation now where you can do everything needed to bring your characters to life. Hardware restrictions on the last generation of consoles were still a bit hard to build convincing 3D characters. With the next generation I don't think there will be any technical limitations left.'

1

LEGEND OF KAY

Modeling, texturing, and rigging 3D characters remains a complex, skilled task. Do you see this changing in the future?
'Valuable tools always made it easier to catch up with the ever-growing demand in technical detail and quality, but the bar will be raised again with the next generation and I think it will always be a challenge to reach a perfect quality.'

How do you work with character design? Is it a specialized area handled by one or a group of artists?
'As productions get bigger and bigger, tasks have to be split and assigned to specialists. On *Legend of Kay* we had a dedicated concept artist focusing only on character design, one in-house lead-character modeler, and an external team working on additional modeling. I expect this is going to split even more as production size increases.'

What do you think about realism in games?
'Realism is a very easy way to get people emotionally involved, but on the other hand it's very hard to design believable realistic characters in games. Players will recognize every wrong little detail in a character's face naturally – something looks wrong – and in that moment the spell is broken.'

What are the most important elements you are looking to achieve both in character design and animation?
'The spark of life. A lot of game characters appear to be dead in some way – something is missing to catch the player's attention and emotional involvement.'

1. More in-game action.
2. Character turnaround sheet.
3. Character creation process.
4. Character sketch of Kay's uncle.
5. The Panda.

1

2

| Rough sketch | | Refined sketch | Colour sketch | Modeling and skinning | Final in-game model |

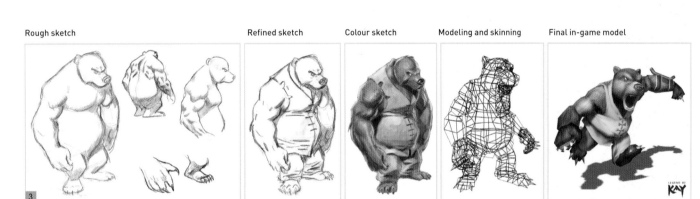

3

4

5

What would you say are the challenges to bringing cartoon characters from a traditionally 2D medium into real-time interactive 3D?

'3D characters can easily look stiff and cold. On paper you have much more freedom to play with perspective and form, the eyes, and facial expressions.'

What's the most fun part of character design and creation?

'Inventing your own worlds and inhabitants and bringing it to life is really great fun. My fascination to create games was always driven by that challenge, but I also love arcade classics like *Asteroids* who don't care about that at all and just blow you away with instant action.'

BIG BICEPS 2

MUSCULAR HEROES

'IT'S TIME TO KICK ASS AND CHEW BUBBLE GUM AND I'M ALL OUT OF GUM.' DUKE NUKEM

SIMPLE CHOICES FOR SIMPLE CHARACTERS. COMPUTER GAMES AND TOUGH GUYS WERE MADE FOR EACH OTHER.
WHERE BETTER FOR TEENAGE BOYS TO INDULGE THEIR POWER FANTASIES WITHOUT RISK TO ANYONE ELSE OR
PULLING A MUSCLE PUMPING IRON AT THE GYM?

Concept drawing from **Street Fighter:
Anniversary** by Capcom's Production Studio 2.

The avenging muscle-bound hero first oiled up for the screen in 1982 with Sylvester Stallone's character John Rambo in the action war movie, *First Blood*. Prior to this you have to look as far back as Greek mythology to find muscle-bound hulks taking the leading role in mainstream literature; otherwise they were usually relegated to the bad guy's grunting henchman.

The muscle-bound hero makes the perfect game character if you view games with the same narrow perspective of much of the industry. They suit the standard hardcore gamer demographic of adolescent boys and young men who prefer to fight it out with aliens in front of a flickering screen rather than gather the nerves to talk to the girl next door. The story is wonderfully simple, too – few need to read further than the first line of back-cover blurb to

guess the rest of the back-story. It's usually revenge for a murdered colleague or a, 'We called you, because you are the best,' save-the-world mission. Duke Nukem has the onerous task of liberating the world's 'babes' from the clutches of alien invaders. Whatever the tale, it always results in an excuse for extensive carnage, the mainstay of the video game. Yet the way these characters are portrayed in games is often as a sniggering postmodern aside. The character designers know they are creating a ridiculous stereotype as much as the players know they are playing it, but both parties can enjoy the comfort of a tried-and-tested gaming paradigm.

Of course, the true history of the muscle-bound hero is to be found in American superhero comics, which stretch back to Superman's debut in the 1930s. These comic heroes, such as

1. **BC** by Intrepid. Prehistory, and a long time before the invention of deodorant. These drawings show the wonderful variety of characters possible, even with a limited wardrobe of a loin cloth and axe.

2–4. Wonderful stretched perspectives give action to these concept sketches for Spike/Dream Factory's beat 'em up, **Crimson Tears**.

5. Pan and Bullet. **Freedom Force** by Irrational Games sported a fabulously huge and inventive variety of original superheroes.

2

2 3
4 5

1

Spiderman and the Fantastic Four, are often far more complex and three-dimensional. When transferred to the game their dialogue balloons are deflated and they are left with only kicking, punching, and flipping across the game-screen, a fraction of their character's true identity. It's a similar, but less important, problem to the loss of laughter that plagues established cartoon characters when they appear in silicon.

For superheroes, however, it works well in one sense, because players, who are also comic fans, will see the game as an entertainment extension of their favourite character. Now, instead of just reading about the action, you get a chance to give it a try, while still enjoying the resonance of the huge back-story established in the comics. It's an example of a character being bigger than any one medium he or she appears in, and showing different facets of their personality in different media. The danger is that many licensed character owners see the game version as a cheap adjunct and put minimum effort into producing a good game, and sadly the superhero has suffered more than most over the years.

Where strongmen have really smashed out a name for themselves is in the beat 'em up genre, and it's here that we see the greatest imaginative variety, where muscles are truly at home. From *Bushido* and *Kung Fu* in 1984, through *Street Fighter* (Capcom, 1987), *Double Dragon,* and *Mortal Kombat* (Midway, 1992), to name but a few, the genre has provided a wonderfully rich seam of interesting characters, many of whom appear, like old friends, from one sequel to the next. Although the game play is restricted to brawling, the characters often have interesting and considered backgrounds that support their appearance and fighting styles.

1. Leo and Dimitri from **Fightin' Jam** by Capcom's Production Studio 2. In the world of the beat 'em up, where there are just two characters in a ring, visual style is important if the game is going to stand out from the crowd.

2–3. **Street Fighter: Anniversary** by Capcom's Production Studio 2. Wonderfully expressive concept drawings that already contain the sense of weight and 3D form that goes into the final in-game models.

2

23

HANDS ON: SOURCES OF INSPIRATION

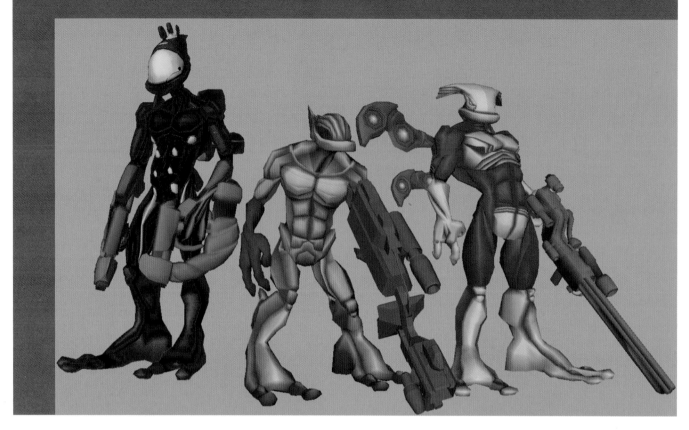

Sometimes it feels as though the world is already overpopulated with fictional characters, to the point that if you were asked to write a list of all the characters you could recall, from any medium, it would no doubt run into hundreds, even thousands. It does seem that with the immense scale, sophistication, and output of the media industries every possible niche of character is already occupied. How is the artist to create an original character who can be heard above this cacophony?

DON'T I KNOW YOU?

Recognized stereotypes and archetypes can have their place in any media and in some situations perform an important function. Indeed, the structure of this book is organized around them. They work as a shorthand method of communication for everyone involved in making the game, from artists to executives, right through to the player buying the box. If you are facing a panel of financiers looking for funding for your game it's easy to say, 'He's like Conan with a beard,' or 'James Bond, but French'.

All present will instantly flick through their collective knowledge of icons to build a character portrait. Everything is already filled in: the character's look, bearing, background, vocation, and possible motivations. For the marketing department, when it comes to hyping the game, they can rely on that same collective knowledge to quickly communicate with the concept to potential purchasers.

The problem is that because stereotypes are well known they hold no surprises. Retreading the same old ground is comforting for executives because it usually guarantees some commercial success but very rarely results in a hit. Blockbusting characters, such as Lara Croft, Max Payne, even Sonic the Hedgehog, were successful partly because they arrived fresh and unexpected into a jaded market.

These images show various stages of development of the game **Alter Echo**, developed by Outrage and published by THQ.

2

STRANGERS

In a world awash with images, it's easy to overlook the rich variety in real life around us. With an enquiring eye, a walk down any main drag offers up an incredibly wide choice of potential game characters to choose from. Of course, back at the drawing board, most will require extensive modification to sit comfortably in your latest beat 'em up or survival horror adventure, but you will find the seed of a character in even the most mundane of fellow humans.

Aside from being a direct source of inspiration, studying those around us helps guard against the creeping blandness that seems to infect many of the more visually realistic games. Characters, for example in the recent crop of WW II adventure games, are cut from a little too-perfect mould. They can often resemble shop dummies whose features have received a superficial tweak, instead of reflecting the huge variety of people we see every day.

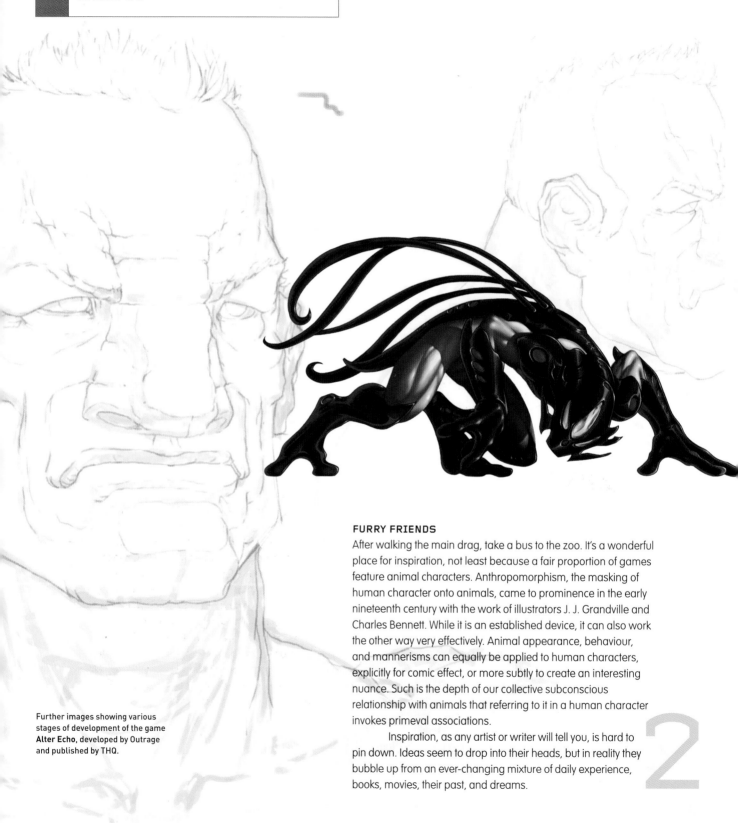

Further images showing various
stages of development of the game
Alter Echo, developed by Outrage
and published by THQ.

FURRY FRIENDS

After walking the main drag, take a bus to the zoo. It's a wonderful
place for inspiration, not least because a fair proportion of games
feature animal characters. Anthropomorphism, the masking of
human character onto animals, came to prominence in the early
nineteenth century with the work of illustrators J. J. Grandville and
Charles Bennett. While it is an established device, it can also work
the other way very effectively. Animal appearance, behaviour,
and mannerisms can equally be applied to human characters,
explicitly for comic effect, or more subtly to create an interesting
nuance. Such is the depth of our collective subconscious
relationship with animals that referring to it in a human character
invokes primeval associations.

Inspiration, as any artist or writer will tell you, is hard to
pin down. Ideas seem to drop into their heads, but in reality they
bubble up from an ever-changing mixture of daily experience,
books, movies, their past, and dreams.

FROM WHERE DO YOU DRAW YOUR INFLUENCES, OTHER GAMES OR OTHER MEDIA?

GILLES BENOIS (CREATOR OF *STARSHOT*, INFOGRAMES)
'From people I know, from people I cross in the street, from characters I like in animated films, actors I like, books and comics I've read .... The video games are too young to propose as many interesting characters as other media do.'

FARZAD VARAHRAMYAN (SAMMY STUDIOS)
'Influences can come from anywhere. Again, listing influences may not be as useful as explaining methodology. We strive to use as much relevant photographic reference as possible that may be appropriate to the character we are designing. I don't care how realistic or alien a design is, you need to visually anchor it. Visual cues are critical to make the audience read into the design and begin to form their own opinions and connections to the character. If you've done your job right, your character design will resonate with most of your audience on some primary and universal levels.'

SIKU (VISUAL DIRECTOR AT ELIXIR STUDIOS, LONDON)
'Never any game, not ever, a strong no, no! I would rather use games to direct me in what not to do. The idea is too unique, isn't it? My influences comes from the great tradition of phenomenal artists before me largely in science fiction and fantasy art, not to mention the great Dutch and Renaissance masters and a couple of some of America's greatest illustrators, notably Leyendecker and Norman Rockwell. There is also a contemporary street sci-fi style out there, born out of the Graffiti-Grunge-Indie music generation. It tends to bend the rules a little. I like looking at stuff like that; they generally tend to be comic-book artists like myself. I find comic book art more inspiring than most contemporary stuff. Of course all media is useful for inspiration.'

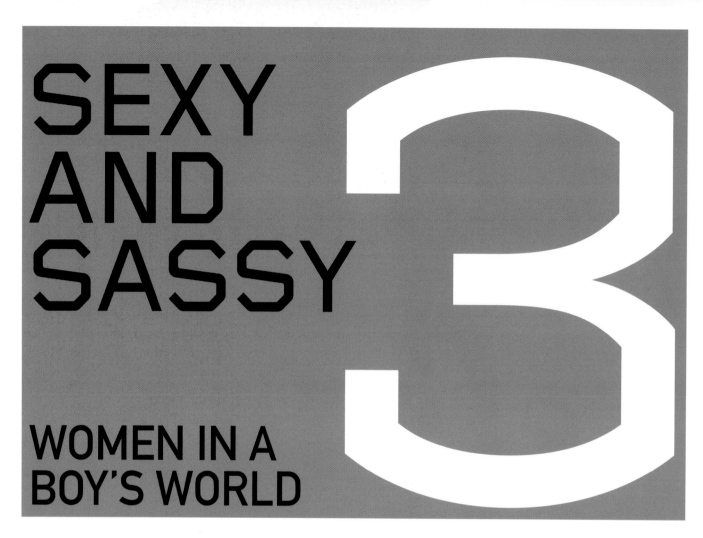

SEXY AND SASSY 3

WOMEN IN A BOY'S WORLD

WHY DO THEY DO IT? WHILE THE GUYS ARE ARMED TO THE TEETH, SNUG IN THEIR BATTLE ARMOUR WITH SENSIBLE SHOES ON, THESE GIRLS ARE WEARING NEXT TO NOTHING AND PERFORMING BALLETIC FLYING KICKS IN FIVE-INCH HEELS. THEY DO IT BECAUSE SEX SELLS.

Eden Studio's **Kya: Dark Lineage.**

Or is it that simple? Yes, if you consider that most games are made by young (and not so young) males with the idea to sell to more young males. As any advertiser will tell you, featuring a beautiful young woman is a sure way to catch the eye of any man, not only the young. If it is this simple it should be subject to some reasonable criticism as the objectification of women. However, while superficially true, look past those iron-clad brassieres and you find a revolution with games at the vanguard.

Artists have portrayed women as nude and semi-dressed throughout history, because it is claimed that the female form is aesthetically beautiful. While the validity of this may be contested on all kinds of levels, it continues to be a fundamental belief of our culture. In the work of artists such as Renoir, Ingres, and Rembrandt, we have seen the feminine form pass through

changing fashions of what is considered beautiful. Currently games tend to take their idea of the perfect woman from fantasy and sci-fi art, a woman who is large-breasted, slim, and physically fit, more or less matching a vogue across all media. The question is, why are they ideals? For the same reason that most men in games are handsome and gym-fit, the game world is an idealized fantasy, like many movies, novels, and TV shows.

However, these pixelated beauties aren't found in their traditional roles at the kitchen sink, or whimpering pathetically as the prey of some snorting predator. These women are out there fighting with as much gusto as the he-men five times their size. Indeed many beat 'em ups put small, delicate, and decoratively dressed schoolgirls in the ring against great sweating hulks. And they are equally matched.

1. **BC** by Intrepid. Prehistoric chic.
2. **Ninja Gaiden** by Team Ninja. A high-resolution render created for marketing.
3. The girls from **Crimson Tears** by Spike/Dream Factory wearing fetishistic bondage gear, a common theme in many games.
4. **Dead or Alive Extreme Volleyball** by Team Ninja. A game that doesn't make any excuses, even the 'wobbly bits' are subject to in-game handling.

3

Looking across all the game genres you find women are included as much as men, and not just for decoration. There are many examples in these pages, such as *Beyond Good and Evil, Kya: the Dark Lineage,* and of course, the queen of them all, *Tomb Raider,* where the woman is the protagonist. Shoot 'em ups, perhaps the most violent and masculine of genres, actually provide an equal number of gun-toting Amazonian characters with which to dive into the fray. Typically women characters are only excluded from simulations of the historical world, such as the battlefront, or modern environments, such as the football field, situations where women were less represented in the real world anyway.

While partially clad women in thigh-high boots still dash around digital dungeons slaying monsters, there is a new breed of more subtle female characters that are designed to appeal both

to male and female players. Jade from Ubisoft's *Beyond Good and Evil* is physically attractive without being overtly sexual and she wears a practical attire more suited to her action-packed antics. Apart from occasionally wielding her staff, she is more interested in using her camera to achieve her aims without recourse to violence. By far her most attractive quality is her personality, which is carefully considered and fully rounded. She is friendly, motivated, occasionally bad-tempered, with a gentle sense of humour. All this combined creates a very realistic character that the player, whether male or female, can connect and bond with.

The depiction of women in computer games has often crossed into sexist debate. No doubt the semi-naked bimbo will still make an appearance, but recent examples, such as a topless BMX cycling game have not met with success, despite featuring realistic physics of the 'wobbly bits'. Even though the majority of players are male and still like a physically ideal female character, they also want as rounded a character as any male star. From a commercial point of view carefully considered female characters are important if the industry wishes to broaden its appeal.

1. Talim from Namco's **Soul Calibur II** has hints of manga in those big eyes.
2. **Monster Hunter** by Capcom's Production studio 1. The restrictions of limited polygons produces a wonderful, energetic style of its own.
3–4. Ulala from **Space Channel 5** by United Game Artists. A wonderfully camp dancing game.
5. Carrie from **Chrome** by Techland. A high-resolution render for marketing.

2

3 4

5

INSIDER SECRETS: THE FEMININE KICK

KYA: THE DARK LINEAGE

Gilles Benois is the Art Director and character designer on Eden Studio's *Kya: Dark Lineage*, an action-adventure game for the Playstation 2. Kya is a tough but lovable girl from Brooklyn searching for her lost brother in a magical world. Along the way she finds herself at the head of a rebellion to free the peaceful Nativs from oppression by the Wolfens.

Kya herself is the modern game girl heroine, as Gilles explains:
'I think Kya is sexy but not vulgar, trendy but not fashion victim, strong but not body-built, smart but not arrogant, pretty but not a bimbo .... Everything in her matches with the world she lives in. She's just the girl we wanted to play with in the universe we created.'

How important are characters to the video game?
'It sure depends on the kind of game you're making, but the "living" things in a game are always the focus of the player (like in a movie or any kind of picture, animated or not): it's a fact that the human eye is always attracted by them before all in a scene, whatever

it is. In a video game where you have to face many dangers and enemies, you may pay a very special attention to the characters and their way to be a part of your virtual world.'

In what ways do you think game characters differ from characters in other media such as movies or literature?
'In a funny way, the main character of a video game is less important than the other ones. Anyone must be able to identify with him. You don't look at him: you are him. In a book or a movie, you can hate a hero. No problem: it's not you, you're not acting. No way in a game: the character must be a part of a phantasm of yours (that's why our characters are often so "smooth" or monolithic and caricatured). The word "avatar" used for the main character shows well that it's a representation of a part of you.'

All images from **Kya: The Dark Lineage.**

3

All images from **Kya: The Dark Lineage.**

What are the special requirements of a game character?

'Smoothness yet charisma, that's all the paradox: you must like him, but everyone else must like him too. The marketing people will require him to be awesome in the selling place and attract everyone, yet the player can be anyone: the point is to repulse no one. It's a fact: you can't please everyone. The most important part is to serve the game play. The basic design must be inducted by his actions. Is he fast? Is he light? Is he smart? What does he have to do in this game? If you take care of the game play, the skeleton of your character will draw itself naturally. Just read carefully the game design: your character is already drawn there .... Contrasted with his enemies, in harmony with the places he'll have to be, well animated (that's extremely important!). Most of all, he must be credible in the situations you want him to be. I insist on the marketing part of the work: if the people selling your game don't like your characters, don't even dream to sell it.'

Who or which games characters do you think are the best?

'When you're OK with the action part of your character, just look at your art direction one more time, you'll see that everything comes naturally. That's why my favourite game character is Link from *Zelda: Wind Waker* (Nintendo) and Yoshi with the little Mario on its back in *Yoshi's Island* (Nintendo). Both are just what they had to be and look really cool.'

How important is the back-story to a game character?

'We all are the result of our experiences. If you want to build a strong character, you must know everything about him, everything about his past. Why do people look much older than they are? Why do you wear those clothes? Have you enough money to get new ones? What about your car? Do you wear glasses? Who are your friends? Do you have some special clothes because of your job? Does your girlfriend buy your clothes for you? It's a never-ending listing, but if you can answer all these questions, you realize that the biggest part is done and that the character already lives and breathes. You just have to put him on the paper.'

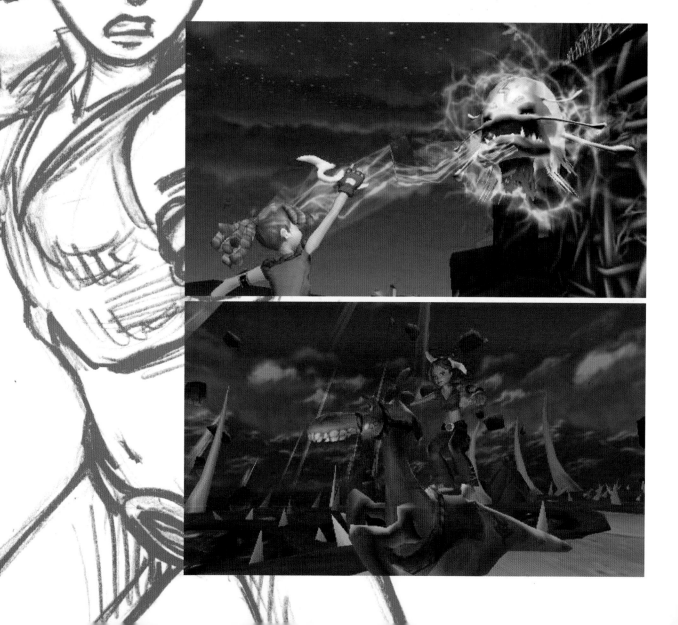

GAME CHARACTER CREATION

RELEVANT AND PRACTICAL ADVICE FROM **SANDY SPANGLER**, NOT ONLY FOR THE GAME ARTIST APPROACHING CHARACTER DESIGN, BUT ALSO FOR THOSE COMMITTEES OF MOVERS AND SHAKERS THAT MAKE THE FINAL DECISIONS. SANDY SPANGLER HAS BEEN CREATING CHARACTERS AND CONTENT IN THE GAMES INDUSTRY FOR MORE THAN TEN YEARS, FIRST AS A LEAD ARTIST AND ANIMATOR AT HUMONGOUS ENTERTAINMENT IN SEATTLE, AND MOST RECENTLY AS A GAME DESIGNER AT ELIXIR STUDIOS IN LONDON.

The majority of modern games contain characters. Some characters the player is supposed to like, some are to be feared and fought against, and some others become an extension of the player. We have been surrounded by characters from stories all of our lives, from fairytales to breakfast cereal boxes – so why is it so difficult to create successful ones for games?

I feel there are two main reasons for this. First of all, creating a good character takes a lot more time and energy than a game production schedule usually allows it; a high-end animated movie studio will spend many months getting a character exactly right, while a game studio rarely prioritizes the process to a similar degree. But when you think about it, a movie character is only on screen for two hours or even less, while a player can spend days or even weeks with a game character. Shouldn't they warrant similar creative attention?

Secondly, I feel that the majority of people working in the games industry have little or no experience in other character-based entertainment media (movie, TV, fiction) and therefore have little knowledge of character and story development outside the

very basic levels that have been accepted by gaming audiences of the past. But if games are to fulfill their potential and embrace a larger, more demanding audience they are going to have to learn a thing or two from the forms of entertainment the world is more familiar with, such as TV and movies, ones that focus on characters and stories. Although computer games have grown into a fledgling storytelling media of their own, their roots remain in ones and zeros – the focus of development is on graphics, game play mechanics, and code. And while I fully acknowledge that ugly graphics or lousy game play cannot be salvaged by interesting characters, the 'creative layer' of a game (subject, setting, story, and style) can be the factor that determines whether or not a potential player picks up your title off a shelf.

1. The **Pajama Sam** series by Humongous Entertainment, 2001. Early concept painting.
Opposite. Back of the envelope sketches including colour swatches.

3

HAIR SAME FROM LEFT EXCEPT FOR OVERLAP LINES

ARMS/LEGS THICKER AT WRISTS/ANKLES

PAJAMA SAM

Sam™ Made Simple!

Add crazy lines.

③ FINISH HIM!

THE GEOMETRY THAT IS SAM

Hair Corner

Use these handy wedges to help you draw Sam's coif when he's at crazy angles.

BUT AVOID THIS!

SEE TOP FOR SIDE VIEW

PUTT PUTT

We have reached a point in the industry where information processing and image display limitations have all but vanished, where dramatic camera sweeps and photo-real textures are everyday occurrences. We now have polygon counts that would make your head swim.

So what's the next step? How can we move into the world of mainstream entertainment media and create consistently engaging characters that do not leave the player feeling hollow?

What follows is a process for character development that attempts to take into account the issues that are common to all character-based media and those that are unique to games. Start by asking yourself the following questions:

What purpose does this character need to fulfil?

Games characters are unique in that they are both characters and tools. They must both elicit the desired response from the player and serve their role within the structure of the game. So the first step in designing a character is to define what is required in order for it to be effective. This list should include:

Mechanical/Game play requirements

What do they need to be able to do? Run, jump, climb, shoot? Define technical limitations that you will have to work within, as well as any limitations set by the game universe (the world is mostly water, there is less gravity, everyone wears roller skates, etc.). Remember that limitations can result in creative and entertaining solutions. Think of the restricted universes in Pixar movies like *A Bug's Life* or *Toy Story*; a rolled leaf with a drop of water became a telescope, a rescue rope was made from a plastic barrel of monkeys.

Necessary communication to the player

What does the player need to know about this character in order to understand the game? Is this a character they should fight? Befriend? Follow? Keep in mind that unexpected outcomes can also make for interesting game play; a terrifying monster that saves your life is much more memorable than one you kill.

3

Personality requirements

What does this character's personality need to be, and what is their role in the story (if there is one)? Is this someone the player should identify with? Fear? Aspire to?

Style consistency

What decisions have been made about the look and feel of the world this character is to inhabit? Is it bright and cartoony, dark and murky, shiny and futuristic? Make sure the character clearly belongs there.

Other media

Where else will this character appear besides this game? Will they appear in a TV show or a movie? If so, they will need a level of

All images on this spread are work in progress concepts from **Warhammer 40,000: Fire Warrior**, developed by Kuju Entertainment and published by THQ. The grim roll-call of portraits from an everlasting future war.

depth that will support future story development. If they have the substance of a cereal mascot, what audience will sit through a two-hour movie?

What *doesn't* this character need to be/do?

Now examine all of the above decisions. Use the undefined areas inbetween the requirements as creative opportunities. When designing a character it is important to remain open-minded and flexible; don't limit yourself unnecessarily by making assumptions. If a character needs to fire a projectile, does it have to be a gun/ bullet? What about a slingshot? A peashooter? A bowling ball? Just because they need to pick things up, do they need to have hands? What about tentacles, a robotic arm, or a toilet plunger? Can they draw things toward them with magnetism? Can they move things with their mind? Innovative game mechanics can often come from unusual characteristics.

To get you started here are my challenges to three common assumptions; whether you agree with them or not, they are worth considering in the name of innovation:

Realism is overrated

Why does everyone in the games industry assume that the more realistic the images they produce, the more engaging they will be? With present technology game developers have the world – any imaginable world, really – at their feet. Why keep presenting the same tired version over and over, especially one that is available right outside the player's door? Why not provide your players with a world that they can escape to, one that without your creative vision they would never experience? In terms of character design, a player's ability to project themselves onto a character is inversely proportional to how specific the image is; a photographic likeness represents only the person in the photograph, but a smiley face can represent anyone in the world. A more stylized and simplified character can take advantage of this.

These characters from Eurocom's **Sphinx and the Shadow of Set** show the rich inventiveness that goes into many games.

Characters do not need to be human to be interesting

Fables use animals as characters for a reason – they are more universally identified with. It is no accident that all of Pixar's feature films to date (*Toy Story I* and *II*, *A Bug's Life*, *Monsters Inc.*, *Finding Nemo*) have no human characters within the core cast. Who is more memorable, Bugs Bunny or Elmer Fudd?

By going outside the human realm you can take advantage of associations people make with animals or objects; a fox character will immediately be thought of as clever and sly, a roadrunner speedy, a book knowledgeable. Human characters are also weighed down with expectations regarding how they would walk, talk, and behave because if there is one thing people are familiar with, it is people; a non-human character opens up a much broader realm of possibility. How would an umbrella stand tap dance? An elephant go bowling? A bunch of broccoli play the violin? You decide.

Character customization is pointless ...

... unless it contributes to game play. A player will be more engaged by your imagination than by their own. The whole point of developing a character is to make the player respond to what makes the character unique – why dilute that experience by giving the player control over clothes, hair, etc.? Yes, there are games where some level of choice might help make the player identify with the character more or make the character recognizable in a group, but this flexibility comes at a price: the more input a player has, the less character there is for them to believe in. Eventually there is no character left, only an avatar – and avatars are not characters, they are on-screen symbols representing the player. The Sims 'characters' are a perfect example; they are incredibly customizable, but because of this they ultimately feel rather soulless.

The characters from Eurocom's *Sphinx and the Shadow of Set* show the rich inventiveness that goes into many games.

How do I engage my audience?

Don't fall into the assumption trap. Consider the player's age range, gender, and interests when designing a character for a specific audience, but don't assume that just because they have bought dozens of games starring big men with guns, for example, that is all they will identify with. Yes, we are in a phase of the industry where big development budgets mean financial risk and alienating your potential buyer could be an expensive mistake, but becoming lost in the bargain bin of 'Me Too' games is equally risky.

A good character will have resonance regardless of its wrapping, so don't be afraid to push the envelope; even if you start with a familiar archetype make sure you take it further and make it uniquely your own. Consider some extremely successful game characters and how they broke the mould: Mario (a pudgy plumber), Sonic (a hedgehog?!?), Guybrush Threepwood (skinny and awkward), Manny Calavera (a 'Day of the Dead' figure), Lara Croft (a powerful woman – gasp!).

3

Who is this character?

In what ways will this character surprise people? Predictable characters are not interesting. When deciding who your character is, be sure you add unexpected aspects to their personality. Indiana Jones was terrified of snakes, Al Capone cried at the opera; what can you add that will give your character complexity?

One way to ensure this is to create a 'character diamond'. The idea is that if you have four main aspects to your character (one on each corner of a diamond) and they all fit together without any contrast, the character will be dull and stereotypical. At least one of the corners of the diamond should oppose the others in order to create conflict and therefore depth. A hero who is strong, clever, brave, and handsome is as dull as a box of rocks; a hero who is strong, clever, handsome, and neurotic or one who is strong,

clever, brave, and ugly is immediately interesting. And for a villain to be truly effective he or she cannot be purely evil, he or she must inspire a grain of empathy; even villains need a soul. (Hannibal Lecter is all the more terrifying because part of you likes him.)

Using this basic framework and all the decisions you have made up until now, write an evocative description of your character. It doesn't have to be especially long, but it should provide a thorough impression of who this character is. It could include anything from their hopes and fears to their least favourite food; include anything that might evoke the right response in the reader.

Here are some basics (but don't limit yourself to these):

Likes and dislikes/Motivations and fears/Strengths and weaknesses/Family history/Race/Species/Gender/Age/Name.

Some of the many characters from Koei's fabulous **Dynasty Warriors** series.

One other thing to keep in mind (especially if the character is part of a story) is character growth. For a story to feel satisfying, the main character must undergo some sort of change before it is over. What growth will your character experience? Will he gain a greater understanding of himself or the world, overcome a long-held fear, turn to the Dark Side? Even if this aspect of his character is not expressed directly in the game, it will help to establish it regardless. A fully developed character takes on a life of his own and will make decisions for you throughout the production process, making your job easier and making them consistent – and therefore believable.

All right, you have a character in your mind. You know who he is and what he would do in any given situation. Now you need to decide what he looks like.

World of Warcraft by Blizzard. MMORPGs open an entirely new scale to games design where we already see tens of thousands of unique player characters. The game worlds themselves may last for many years, evolving their own digital cultures, ways of life, and family trees.

Follow through with your intent

In character design nothing is an accident. All aspects of a character should be there for a reason, either to meet an established requirement (game play or otherwise) or to help communicate the character's personality. Don't just give him/her arbitrary features, it will undermine the character's integrity and dilute the strength of the features that do mean something.

At this stage you should not only be thinking in terms of a character's appearance expressing their purpose and personality – what will he sound like? How will he move? Gather as much source material as possible for costumes, colour schemes, and accessories, as well as sound and motion. (The motion reference will also be useful later on when you get to the animation phase – if a villain is supposed to 'move like a crab' it will make the animator's job a lot easier if you can show him what you have in mind. Same goes for sound reference and voice casting.)

3

053

Create concept art

Less is not more – more is more. The more concept drawings that can be generated, the better, with as much variety as possible. A true concept artist has a flexible style and can create dozens of very different versions of a character. If the artists at your disposal have a stronger and more limited style, select styles that are closest to what is needed for the game and use as many artists as you can. At a game company I used to work for, during the concept phase the Lead Artist would send out an email to all the artists in the company listing the new characters and a description of each. When artists had some spare time or needed a break from their regular work they would crank out some concept sketches and post them in a selected hallway. That way everyone could see what different characters people were coming up with, which would then trigger more new ideas. After a few weeks the walls were covered with a broad range of concept art.

The character concept-art cycle

1 Generate the first round of sketches. These should be rough but expressive, and should be created very quickly with lots of variety.

2 Narrow down which ones have features that work well ('I like this hair, but not that nose,' etc.). Get multiple opinions on this to help ensure broad appeal.

3 Do another round of drawings, a bit tighter this time and combining the features that were selected from round one. (At this point you don't need a whole army of artists, just a few whose styles work with the game.)

4 Repeat steps 2 and 3 until you have a 2D version of the character that seems to work well (expect at least three or four rounds of artwork, not including colour tests). The final version should include colour and a 'turnaround' view showing the character's front, back, and side.

3

5 Once you have the design you like, get feedback on it if possible, either through focus testing or at the very least, internal company review. Make any needed adjustments in response to the feedback. But do not design by committee! One or two people, usually the Lead Artist and/or Lead Designer, must have the final say.

6 The last step is to put the character into its final state; for computer games this probably means modelled and textured in 3D. The evolution from 2D drawing to 3D character is fraught with artistic peril, however; be very careful that the character's integrity and appeal are maintained.

In closing …
Don't be afraid to give character development the time and energy it deserves. And don't be afraid to go back to the drawing board if a character you have created just isn't working. If a character is effective, players will remember it long after the game play has ended. From a practical standpoint this maximizes the potential success of sequel games as well as a possible future in other media. From a cultural standpoint you will be providing a richer and more meaningful game play experience for thousands, possibly even millions of people, as well as making a positive contribution to modern mythology. It's high time we in the games industry took some responsibility for that.

Remember, characters should ultimately come from the heart, not a spreadsheet. Because game characters must have a practical, functional side it is all too easy to let them be nothing more than an on-screen tool – it is up to you to take them further. If you, their creator, don't understand their inner workings and believe in them, no-one else will either. The world is full of empty characters; do not create more of them.

Jowood Productions' **Neighbours from Hell** has an interesting claymation style of rendering.

MAD, BAD, AND DANGEROUS TO KNOW

4

BYRONIC HEROES

'APART HE STALK'D IN JOYLESS REVERIE. AND FROM HIS NATIVE LAND RESOLV'D TO GO, AND VISIT SCORCHING CLIMES BEYOND THE SEA; WITH PLEASURE DRUGG'D HE ALMOST LONG'D FOR WOE.'

CHILDE HAROLD'S PILGRIMAGE, CANTO 1. LORD GEORGE GORDON NOEL BYRON, 1812

THIS WAS THE FIRST APPEARANCE OF THE BYRONIC HERO IN BYRON'S WORK, EVEN THOUGH THE CHARACTER CAN BE IDENTIFIED WANDERING THROUGH EARLIER ENGLISH ROMANTIC LITERATURE. 'MAD, BAD, AND DANGEROUS TO KNOW' COMES FROM LADY CAROLINE LAMB'S OBSERVATION OF LORD BYRON, WHO, AFTER CREATING THE FICTIONAL CHARACTER, VERY MUCH PLAYED THE PART HIMSELF.

Hitman by I.O. Interactive. The really creepy extreme of the Byronic hero, a man who has become disconnected from his emotions.

From those early Gothic novels to modern computer games, the Byronic hero is an outsider, wanting to be virtuous, but dragged into darker realms by his irrepressible passions. To his lover he is devoted, but equally unfaithful. He can show kindness, and in turn, cruelty. He must constantly move on, forever seeking new sensations. Women find his lack of fidelity repellent but are irresistibly drawn to his fiery passion and intense good looks. We see him most famously as Heathcliff in Emily Bronte's *Wuthering Heights*, 1847, and on the silver screen as the rebellious bike gang leader, Johnny Strabler, in *The Wild One*, 1953. In novels he is a fascinating and complex character who has arrived in the different format of the computer game with interesting results.

Perhaps his earliest digital outing was as Gabriel Knight in Jan Jenson's *Gabriel Knight: The Sins of the Fathers* (1993, Sierra). The game had quite a star-studded voice cast with Tim Curry (Gabriel), Leah Remini (Grace), Mark Hamill (Det. Mosely), and Michael Dorn. Gabriel was a classic Byronic hero, complete with the propensity to chase women.

In the *Eternal Darkness* series all of the 12 characters you play can become susceptible to madness and inflamed emotions as a function of the game play, through the sanity meter. If your character's sanity drops too low as a result of witnessing gruesome crimes the character becomes unpredictable and harder to control, in effect becoming the Byronic hero.

1–2. **Max Payne 2: The Fall of Max Payne** by Remedy. Max Payne is a classic Byronic figure. Torn apart by his family's brutal murder, he goes around hunting down those responsible for the murder, riding roughshod over police guidelines.

3–5. **Metal Gear Solid** series by Konami. The bearded Snake at work in the field.

4

The back-story is suitably Gothic, centring around the Roivas family and its relationship with an ancient book, *The Tome of Eternal Darkness*. As a player you step into the skin of one of each of the Roivas family generations. This in itself is a fascinating opportunity to experience the different ages through the eyes of contemporary characters, including their attitudes and outlook.

Metal Gear Solid, which was first seen in 1988, features a tough, James Bond-like character called Solid Snake. Like Bond, he operates to his own rules, is a cunning loner, and, when necessary, a ruthless killer. Throughout the series he becomes embroiled in a series of complex and convoluted missions that eventually focus on his very own reason for being.

What is interesting is that to support a Byronic hero the game must have a strong back-story that interweaves with the character's own life. In fact a strong story and dramatic framework is absolutely necessary to fulfill the requirements of his character traits, with the result that only the adventure game genre can successfully carry him.

Perhaps the most compelling aspect of the character is the tension generated between him and the player. Usually game characters are steered like puppets by the player but the Byronic hero, with a characteristic disregard for authority, struggles free from his strings to be unpredictable and sometimes unlikable. This in itself challenges the player and points the way forward for the industry to design games that allow characters to have their own rich identity – after all, that's why we are drawn to the movies or pick up a novel.

1. **Hitman.** Knowing what a cold-blooded killer he is makes this a most disturbing image.
2–7. **Eternal Darkness** by Silicon Knights. The game was a serious and successful attempt to involve the player, through the characters, in a rich, absorbing, and genuinely creepy story.
8. **Gabriel Knight 3.** Sierra Studios. Gabriel struggling with his Byronic internal turmoil.
9. **Max Payne** by Remedy. Cut scenes used fragments of comic strip to move the story along.

4

INSIDER SECRETS: SHOOTOUT IN GHOST TOWN

DARKWATCH: CURSE OF THE WEST

Farzad Varahramyan is the Creative Visual Director at Sammy Studios. Before joining Sammy Studios, Farzad served as the senior production designer at Oddworld Inhabitants, where he worked closely with Lorne Lanning in creating the *Oddworld* universe. *Darkwatch: Curse of the West* is a sci-fi western first-person shooter starring Jericho Cross in a battle for his life against a gang of vampires and decaying zombies.

In what ways do you think game characters differ from characters in other media such as movies or literature?
'Generally speaking, in film or television, you are a bystander watching the characters go through the chain of predetermined events that define the story. In video games you have an active role in determining the character's decisions, actions, and the outcomes to the story. In most cases you become or project yourself upon that character in the game. Game characters have special requirements in order to work for the medium: readability. A basic necessity but an important one. Expressive in animation and sound for real-time communication. Appeal to gamers – they must be characters that

your target audience should want to "be". Characters can get very stale unless they have an interesting visual hook.'

What are the special requirements of a game character?
'In my opinion, a game character needs to fulfill five main areas. It needs to embody and visually convey the characteristics defined by the story script. It needs functionally to be able to accomplish the game-design requirements it is asked to do. It needs visually to be unique, memorable, and hopefully stand the test of time. It should work as an evocative image on a poster, but also be graphically designed to read well, be recognizable for the type of game it is in, and adhere to limitations of the hardware and software. Personally, I also feel it's successful if someone looks at the character design and asks when the action figure or statue is coming out.'

1. Jericho Cross.
2. Jericho.
3–4. Some of the unsavoury characters Jericho has to deal with.
5. Cassidy.

2 3
4 5

What extra qualities make a game character stand out?

'Visually speaking, I feel you need to have a character design that has a certain graphic signature about it. Basically the average person should view the character, and at a later time be able to recall it, and have it recognized by a friend by describing a dominating visual feature to which the friend can respond, "Oh yes. I know who you are talking about." That feature can be the colours, the silhouette, the pose, the graphics, or a specific symbol on the character, a particular accessory, hairstyle, and the list goes on. If you do your job well, you can use all of the above-mentioned features to layer in uniqueness, tell a story about the character, set a personality, and create a signature look. I also feel if the character sticks out from the crowd and is basically memorable than you've done something right. You've achieved further success if the character has depth and it retains the audience's prolonged interest, curiosity, and long-term willingness to find out more about it.'

What do you find is the most fun part of character design?

'Personally, one of the most gratifying parts of the process is the iteration process. This is where you draw and draw and test and get feedback and then draw some more. This is where you are truly conceiving and creating the character. This is where you breathe life, history, personality, and purpose into a new character. Doing the cool renderings and illustrations can be gratifying too, but this is eye candy that comes after the fact. To show a raw sketch and have people immediately connect to the character you are showing them, that is truly gratifying.'

Oddworld is a world away from *Darkwatch*. How was the switch from Abe to Jericho?

'*Oddworld* was an amazing universe to unravel, visually develop, and expand. It was here where I learned the importance of integrating story and character into game design. Going from developing for *Oddworld* to developing *Darkwatch* and specifically to Jericho, meant going from a humorously and ironically loaded universe to a more mature genre such

4

2

3

1. Jericho on the empty street.
2–3. More of Jericho's adversaries.

as horror. *Darkwatch* also has more mature themes such as romance and love, which did not exist in the asexual *Oddworld* universe. You may say I had some growing up to do.

'You can almost see my own growth process from my development sketches of Jericho. I very much started with what I was used to, that is to develop humorous parodies, applying it to well-known Western icons. As I iterated on the character of Jericho I discovered that I went from wanting to "see" Jericho in the game, to wanting to "be" Jericho in the game. Who would you rather be in a first-person shooter, a goofball, or a badass? You can see from the sketches when the turning point occurred and why Jericho looks the way he does in his present state.'

How much does the story feed into your work and your work into the story?

'When collaborating on the creation of any character, it is critical to have a healthy back and forth with the game designer or scriptwriter. Coming up with the story is critical for laying at least the beginnings of a character design. Conversely, once some images start appearing on paper, they may start to influence and trigger some new story points and ideas. I find this healthy correspondence between writers and concept artists ultimately yields the best stories and character designs.'

How do you make a horror game character really scary?

'We usually add fangs! I'm just kidding ... it's only partly true. For *Darkwatch* we are creating archetypal Western character icons with a series of enemies that are easily recognizable as classic gunslingers, banditos, braves, and undertakers, but all with a *Darkwatch* twist. We also are dealing with creating easily recognizable targets for shooting, so granular subtleties on the character will not be able to carry the load by themselves. The paper designs and 3D model will take it part of the way. Animation, clever AI, good game design, FX, and sound are essential to taking it the rest of the way. Something may be scary-looking on paper but when you get it moving and you are shooting at it, it may not always work as you intended. Be prepared to iterate.'

4

1-2. Demons from Terminal Reality's
Blood Rayne.

FEMME FATALE 5

BAD GIRLS

'THERE OUGHTA BE A LAW AGAINST DAMES WITH CLAWS!'

CHARLIE HASKELL (EDMUND MACDONALD), *DETOUR* (1945)

SHE IS A HONEY TRAP. SHE LURES FOOLISH, LOVESTRUCK MEN INTO DOING HER EVIL BIDDING. THE MEN COME, HYPNOTIZED BY HER FEMININE, EROTIC GUILE, THEIR WILLS CRUMBLED TO DUST BEHIND THEM, AS SHE GUIDES THEM TO THEIR DOOM.

Final Fantasy X-2.

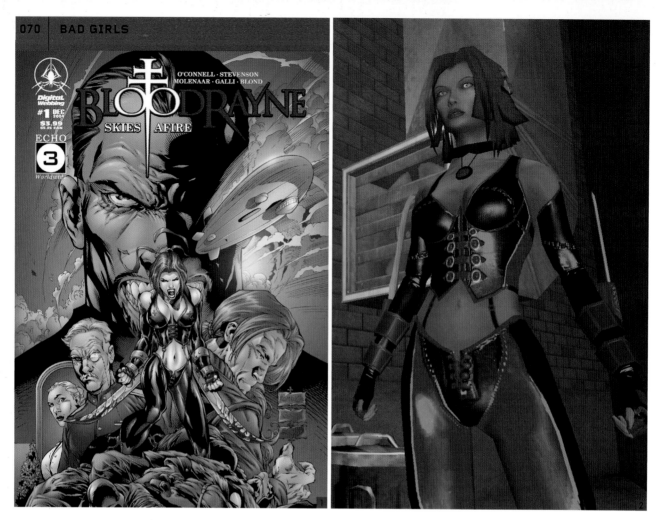

'WHEN I'M GOOD, I'M VERY GOOD. BUT WHEN I'M BAD, I'M BETTER.' MAE WEST

She has woven her way through history from classic mythology to today's video games. In *The Odyssey*, Odysseus and his sailors had to avoid the Sirens, whose irresistibly alluring songs would have taken them to their deaths. She appears in early Judeo-Christian culture in a number of characters such as Eve, Delilah, and Salome, she who demanded the head of John the Baptist.

Where the femme fatale really got her claws in was as the leading lady in the film noir of the 1940s and 1950s. Films such as *Detour* (1945) feature Ann Savage who plays Vera, a hitchhiker who entangles both her ride, Al Roberts (Tom Neal), and herself in an 'accidental' murder. There are many other examples – *Scarlet Street*

(1945), *The Locket* (1947), and *Angel Face* (1953) – to name but a few, but Hollywood had imprinted the visual stereotype: beautiful, dark-haired, with those sleepy 'come-to-bed' eyes.

We see her in computer games in a number of different guises. The first is as a fully rounded character emerging from a believable back-story, the best example of which is *System Shock* and its sequel *System Shock 2* (Looking Glass Technologies and Irrational Games, 1994 and 1999). This femme appears as an out-of-control artificial intelligence which the player is charged with destroying. She has taken control of the Citadel's computers, killed the staff, and programmed the robots to do her bidding. She is terrifyingly omniscient, seemingly able to predict and counter the player's every move.

The most famous of game women, Lara Croft, star of the *Tomb Raider* series, holds some of the classic femme fatale's traits, namely her feisty independence mixed with an alluring, if somewhat over-inflated, physique. And of course she has no

1. The **Blood Rayne** comic. **Blood Rayne** shows the marketing power of the character to transcend any single product.
2. **Blood Rayne** by Terminal Reality and Majesco is both terrifying and seductive.

Opposite. Shahdee from **Prince of Persia** by Ubisoft Montreal. Of course game characters are a lot less subtle than the screen goddesses of film noir, but then games are usually about action so there's little time for long, seductive dialogue.

5

1

2

3

qualms about shooting anyone in her way. Lara embodies the new feminism, the can-do woman who is also in charge of her sexuality.

Another version of the archetype that can be loosely attached to game characters is the girl you can fight with, in games such as *Quake* and *Unreal Tournament*. These women adhere to the concept as the 'Vamp', a character at the extreme end of the femme fatale archetype that draws its influences from the fetish scene of bondage power games. An early example was Red Lotus from Asylum Studios' *Deathtrap Dungeon* (1997) who was dressed in the now-regulation leather bodice and studded halter neck.

Perhaps the most extreme of all game vamps is Terminal Reality's *Blood Rayne*, a half-human, half-vampire child of a vampire father. She is driven to destroy the vampires and avenge her mother's rape by hunting down her father. Blood Rayne is a femme

fatale on max, truly a woman to fear. She goes to work dressed in the most erotic bondage gear, with five-inch heels she uses like talons and fingernail blades for – literally – dicing up her foe.

The fact that in these games you play the part of the femme fatale says a lot about how the femme fatale is regarded today. When she was at large in the film noir she was considered an evil, almost devil-like woman, leading men to their downfall by manipulating their flaws. Today she is as dangerous as ever, but her strength, independence, and drive are seen as positives, especially in the morally neutral environment of the video game. Then again, I suspect this analysis is a little forgiving. The usual perspective for play is third-person so the player, typically male, has a roving eye just behind the heroine. What better view for appreciating her feminine curves, especially as she is safely locked away in the screen?

1. Concept from **The Lord of the Creatures** by Arvirago.
2. **SMT: Digital Devil Saga** by Altus Software. A terrifying female from the sci-fi fantasy RPG based on designs by the artist Kazuma Kaneko.

3. The thief character from Elixir's **Evil Genius.** The femme fatale is beautiful, sexy, and, above all, smart.
4. Lara Croft. **Tomb Raider** by Core.
5–6. Tala from **Darkwatch** by Sammy Studios. Darkwatch mixes biker black

leather, the Wild West, and gothic.
7. The cover painting from Looking Glass' **System Shock 2.**
8. An evil boss character from Team Ninja's adventure, **Ninja Gaiden** is bizarre and strangely beautiful.

5

HANDS ON: CONCEPT ART

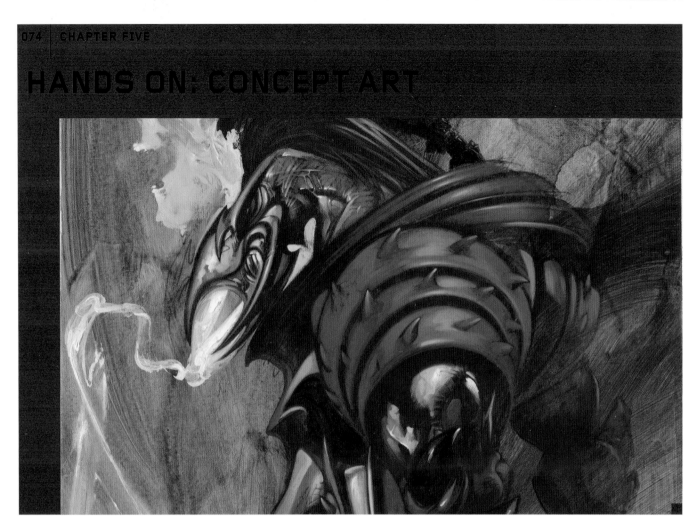

Game companies are at last beginning to see the value of pre-production concept drawing and now employ full-time concept artists. Sadly, however, they are rarely valued as the core generators of valuable concepts, which in turn can become valuable IPs. The task of the concept artist, along with the writer, is central to the entire project, affecting its early ability to raise working capital, through the efficiency of production, to its selling power on the shelf.

REASONS FOR DRAWING 1, 2, 3
EXPLORING AND ORGANIZING IDEAS
A period of experimentation at the start of a huge project like a computer game is critical because if the foundation concepts are flawed, millions can be lost when the game finally goes on sale and flops. In this context a few weeks of a concept artist's time are cheap if it means that a set of characters are devised that are coherent with each other, the story, and the game world, and are right for the intended market.

COMMUNICATION
Drawing up concepts of characters is important for communication both up and down the line. In the first instance it helps the team who come up with the ideas to settle on designs that may go forward. Just a session or two of sitting together sketching and discussing can rapidly find solutions everyone is happy with. However, there is an important rider to this, in that these discussions should be inside the creative team alone. Involving marketing, management, company directors, or more than a handful of contributors will inevitably extinguish the creative spark, reducing any characters devised to dull, focus-group failures. Further down the line the drawings become an important reference for the 3D and textures artists, and paintings provide a focus for everyone involved to share the vision.

5

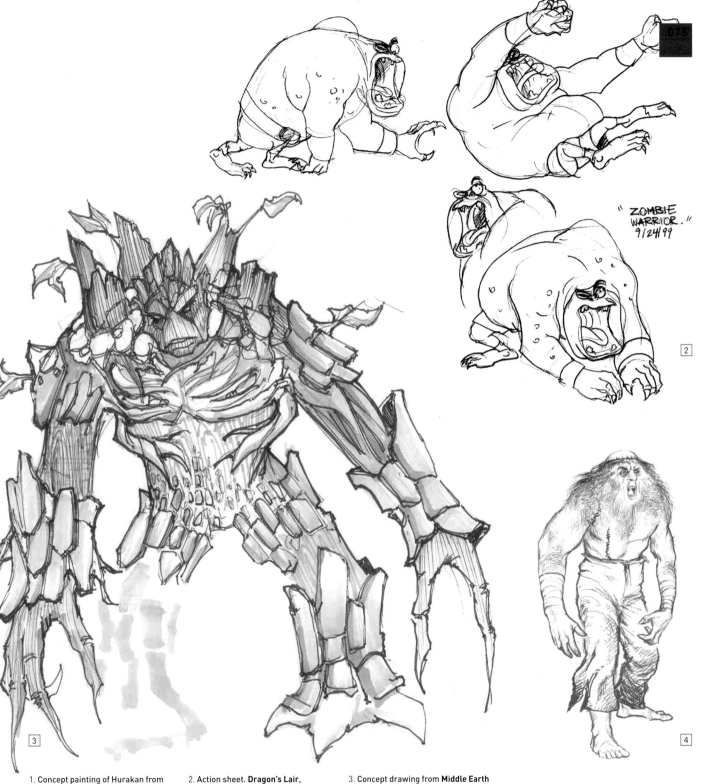

"ZOMBIE
WARRIOR."
9/24/99

2

3

4

1. Concept painting of Hurakan from Elixir's **Blue Vault.**

2. Action sheet. **Dragon's Lair**, developed by Dragonstone Software, is famous for its early high-quality animation by Don Bluth, a star among traditional animators.

3. Concept drawing from **Middle Earth Online** by Turbine.

4. Concept drawings by fantasy artist Martin Mckenna for **Frankenstein's Legions.**

1

FINANCIAL TOOLS

Proof of your idea is essential when projects are at an early stage of development. Going to finance meetings with a verbal pitch and a stack of figures isn't enough, especially in such a visual industry as games. You will need sketches, artwork, and mocked-up screens at the very least. When it comes to selling the game, sketches and finished paintings are ammunition for the marketing people to get the game noticed.

THE DRAWING PROCESS

It's always tempting to miss this part of character creation and dive straight into building models in 3D; after all, you may already have a complete character finished and ready to roll in your head. The chances are, however, that if you try and focus those ideas, they are actually a soup of disjointed, ever-changing visions. Committing them to 3D would be foolish; the medium is too exacting to allow for experimentation.

CHARACTERS AND STORY

Begin sketching at the very beginning of the game concept while the story, indeed the whole idea of the game, is still fluid. The characters are not just part of the story, they *are* the story.

AVOIDING STEREOTYPES

Put your first drawing in a drawer. Typically it will be a stereotype. For example, think of a cook, and the idea of a big, fat sweaty guy in a white apron comes to mind. Eventually it may be right for the part, but it's always worth trying many different body types.

1. **S.T.A.L.K.E.R.: Shadow of Chernobyl** by GSC Game World. A wonderful sheet of mutants that look as though they've sprung from the mind of the late Gothic painter, Hieronymus Bosch.

2. A character sheet from **Middle Earth Online** by Turbine.
3. A character turnaround from I.O. Interactive's **Freedom Fighters**.

5

EXAGGERATION FOR THE SMALL SCREEN

If you are working with realistic characters it's worth giving them slightly more exaggerated features than you would think necessary, almost bordering on cartoon, if you are to avoid the same lifeless, predictable, cardboard cut-out hero that seems to pop up in every other game. Even among the beautiful people, Hollywood stars, there are huge variations in physical appearance. Average features are also somewhat lost on the small screen, because the character usually appears quite small in play rather than in the closer, head-and-shoulder shots seen in TV shows.

ACTING THE PART

Step inside the character, get up and act them out, how they walk, would sit down, get flustered, or swing a sword. They are a combination of so many little traits, habits, and gestures, and thinking of this whole will produce a more convincing character.

TURNAROUNDS

Once you've settled on a character you need to draw up a 'turnaround'. These are common in the animation industry but less often seen in games. Basically, they are the character as seen in three views, from the front, side, and back. Height measurements should also be included, as well as drawings of any equipment, baggage, clothes, etc., that they will be carrying. It's also a good idea to draw the head from a number of different angles and with a collection of expressions.

ACTION POSES

Action sketches are particularly important for cartoon characters because of the wide variety of poses they may get into. The limits of any stretching or compression of the character will have to be discussed with the 3D artists and animators to take into account the constraints of the 3D game engine.

THE RELUCTANT HERO

6

IT'S A BUM RAP

'DON'T EVERYONE THANK ME AT ONCE.' HAN SOLO, *STAR WARS* (1977)

THERE YOU WERE, JUST KEEPING YOUR HEAD DOWN, GETTING ON WITH YOUR WORK WHEN, WHAM! A METEOR HITS YOUR HOUSE, ALIENS ABDUCT THE CAT, YOUR GIRLFRIEND RUNS OFF WITH THE POSTMAN, AND YOU ARE THE ONE GUY THAT HAPPENS TO KNOW HOW TO STOP THE EARTH HURTLING INTO THE SUN. SAVING THE WORLD — WHAT A DRAG.

The cel-shaded **Breath of Fire: Dragon's Quarter** by Capcom. The game's hero, Ryu, is cursed with a dragon's powers that threaten to destroy him while he attempts to save the life of Nina, a waif-like girl with wings who is slowly suffocating in the stifling atmosphere of the world, Sheldar.

The ordinary guy has found himself the hero many times through the years. A few obvious examples are Han Solo in *Star Wars* (1997), Neo in *The Matrix* (1999), and Frodo in *Lord of the Rings*.

Generally there are two types of reluctant hero. One is the victim of circumstance who has to drop whatever he is doing and deal with the problem. The most explicit example can be found in the disaster movie where the character's world is turned upside down. It's quite straightforward, a choice between life and the abyss, resulting in the perfect dramatic opener. The hero in this situation is simply surviving, and how he or she fares becomes the thread of the tale. The most pared-down example would be Robinson Crusoe, who, until Friday appears, is pitted one-on-one against nature.

The other type of reluctant hero is far more interesting because he or she is all about relationships and change of character. The story typically begins with the character being outside or on the periphery of the narrative's dramatic event, getting on with his or her own thing. By 'event' I am referring to anything from a family tiff to a full-scale military invasion. The most selfish may be aware of the event, may even be colluding in it, but for the majority of characters, the initial motive is to avoid becoming involved.

The 'relationships' occur because the character is called upon to help someone for whom the event is a real problem. Perhaps initially they do it for cash, a favour, or even for the chance of romance. Once involved, the reluctant hero begins to understand

1. **Beyond Good and Evil** by Ubisoft. Jade and her pig-human uncle, P'jay, expose treachery. The game enjoys a rich blend of different gameplay styles held together by a strong story.

2. Half-caste human-devil Dante is mankind's only hope against the reawakening of a Devil Emperor. Capcom's **Devil May Cry** displays a beautifully designed world with fast and stylish character animation.

3. Ashe, from the role-playing **Final Fantasy XII** by Square Enix, produced and directed by game-maker guru, Yasumi Matsuno, finds herself cast reluctantly into the part of heroine.

2

3

and empathize with the plight of those in need of his or her help. Finally, the hero realizes that the experience has changed him or her for the better.

The wonderful aspect of a reluctant hero is that he or she doesn't have to adhere to any stereotype, such as being incredibly strong or a trained kung-fu master. These can be average guys off the street; indeed, it's often their simple, homespun down-to-earth thinking that saves the day. This ordinariness is an important factor in allowing the audience to understand and bond with the hero.

How can a reluctant hero work in a computer game beyond a few lines of back-story on the CD case? Surely the whole idea of the game is that the player bought it to become involved

in dangerous situations from the safety of the armchair. What's the point if your character is reluctant to go adventuring? In many games, 'character' is really just a misnomer for a puppet the player steers around. If the character has any *real* character he or she will turn around and challenge the player's decisions. With the character exhibiting some reluctance to accept the player's control, the germ of a relationship is established. A new layer of game play is introduced, that of nurturing a successful relationship. Perhaps more rewarding than completing the game itself?

1. Terrorists or freedom fighters? Character concepts of guerilla fighters in I.O. Interactive's **Freedom Fighters.**

2–3. Tough cop Tanner from **Driv3r** by Reflections Interactive is dragged into investigating a dangerous group of car thieves. A screen showing the incredible realism currently achievable, and a storyboard clip used to plan cut-scene sequences.

4. **ICO** by Sony Computer Entertainment is one of the most beautiful and engaging games ever created. ICO is a 12-year-old abandoned in a giant castle by his community because of his unusual horns.

ARABIAN ARTS: THE PRINCE OF PERSIA

The Prince was first seen leaping across game screens back in 1989 in the 2D classic designed and programmed by Jordan Mechner. Even though it was part of an already established genre, the platform game, it was revolutionary in its fluid character animation and fiendishly devious traps. The story was classic *Arabian Nights* and refreshingly romantic: you played the lovestruck Prince who must free the object of his affections, the Sultan's daughter, from the clutches of the evil Grand Vizier Jaffar. Against time you had to navigate the Prince through the palace corridors deftly leaping, clambering, and somersaulting past a series of cunning traps to save her from the Vizier's deceitful marriage plans.

The character animation was the first use of rotoscoping in game design. Jordan filmed his brother performing the game's various movements and traced them into the Prince's animation. What was striking about the game was its adherence to the rich imagery and atmosphere of the original *Arabian Nights*, rather than pandering to the usual pale and sugar-coated version

1. Screen from **Prince of Persia: Warrior Within.**
Opposite. Concept painting from **Prince of Persia: Warrior Within.**

proffered by Disney. Even with the simple graphics of 8-bit computing, the game had an aesthetic beauty rarely seen since across the entire industry.

The Prince also appeared in the follow-ups *The Shadow and the Flame* and *Prince of Persia 3D*. The latest sequels, *The Sands of Time* and *Warrior Within* have made use of graphics hardware improvements to give our hero a fully realized 3D world to explore. With Jordan consulting on the new series, the developers have created a game that recreates the mystery and splendour of medieval Persia. They have produced a unique style that is reminiscent of the romantic paintings and engravings of eighteenth- and nineteenth-century European travellers on Grand Tours of the Middle East. The Prince himself is now capable of fabulous acrobatics, which can be enjoyed in slow-motion replays using the magical control of time in the game play. In the company of a few select game characters he is weathering the effects of time well by establishing a successful intellectual property that will deservedly translate into other media. What *Prince of Persia* proves is the importance of the single vision in an industry that often misunderstands and disregards its creative geniuses.

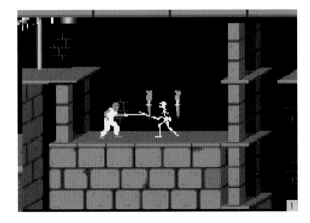

1. The original **Prince of Persia**.
Other images. Concept paintings from
Prince of Persia: The Sands of Time
and **The Warrior Within**.

FASCINATING FLAWS

THE ANTI-HERO

'NOBODY TELLS ME WHAT TO DO. YOU KEEP NEEDLIN' ME, IF I WANT TO,

I'M GONNA TAKE THIS JOINT APART AND YOU'RE NOT GONNA KNOW WHAT HIT YOU.'

JOHNNY STRABLER (MARLON BRANDO), *THE WILD ONE*, 1953.

WHY IS IT THAT THE BAD GUY ALWAYS SEEMS TO HAVE ALL THE FUN? HOLDING UP BANKS, BREAKING THE SPEED LIMIT,

SHOOTING UP COPS, SNEERING AT THE SCHOOLMASTER, RAISING ZOMBIE ARMIES, EVEN INVADING COUNTRIES.

IN THE GAMING WORLD, WHERE MORALITY IS TURNED ON ITS HEAD, ANYONE CAN PLAY THE VILLAIN.

Nightmare from Namco's **Soul Calibur 2.**

1

There are two views of the anti-hero, based on how they are presented to the audience, the first of which contains a wide spectrum of types. At the milder end of the spectrum you might have the Byronic heroes mentioned earlier in the book. Towards the centre you find the character who is essentially good but struggles with a personality flaw. You could go as far back as Achilles from Homer's *Iliad* or Gollum from J.R.R. Tolkien's *Lord of the Rings*. Gollum suffers directly from a split personality; a conflict between good and evil.

Lurking at the darker end are psychotic characters, such as Hannibal Lecter from *Silence of the Lambs*. They border on pure evil, but the hero – bent on his or her defeat – knows, as the audience does, that he or she suffers delusions caused by mental illness. Essentially, these characters, however complex or compelling, are not, in terms of traditional storytelling, the intended heroes of the piece.

The other view of the anti-hero is far more straightforward, where, pure and simple, the hero is the bad guy. The idea of encouraging the audience to follow, and even applaud villainy,

is a relatively modern and controversial theme. Perhaps the best example from the movies would be Oliver Stone's *Natural Born Killers* (1994), which depicts a young couple on a motiveless killing spree. The movie isn't pure, unadulterated violence for its own sake, but rather makes an important point about how the media makes celebrities of criminals.

The *Grand Theft Auto* series by Rock Star Games caused a huge stir with the release of each iteration. From a moral standpoint, and according to the media, it has no redeeming features at all. As a player you control a criminal in a freeform city environment where you can indulge in violent criminal behaviour, including punching old ladies, running down innocent pedestrians,

1. **Grand Theft Auto: Vice City.** Rockstar Games.
2. Villains from **Starsky and Hutch,** developed by Mind's Eye.
3–4. Lucifer and Hikawa from Atlus Software's **Shin Megami Tensei: Nocturne.**

5. In Capcom's stylish action thriller, **Killer 7,** you control Harman Smith, a wheelchair-bound man who is able to physically morph into seven different and deadly anti-heroes. Here we see Coyote Smith and Mask de Smith character sheets.

7

2

3

4

5

gunning down police, and running and reversing your car over prostitutes to avoid paying for services you've just enjoyed. For each crime you are awarded points and although eventually the police will catch you, the corrupt judiciary have you back on the streets in a single loading screen. Apart from a few bandwagon copies and a tiny handful of cult comics, the game stands alone across all media as uniquely morally unrestrained.

The series, particularly *Vice City* and *San Andreas*, has been hugely successful. The feared upsurge in criminal activity as a result of playing has not materialized. However, the game does highlight an interesting point about the player's relationship with game characters

compared to other media. In *GTA*, as the player, you directly control the character, making his decisions, and the fact that you can indulge in criminal behaviour is a function of the game world. Watching a crime in a movie, if the movie is any good, will have some emotional impact on the viewer because the events are being controlled by the screenwriter who makes the viewer care about the protagonists.

Roaming the streets of *Vice City* randomly killing passers-by, the player's character contains no emotional depth, underscored by the fact that a quick restart cheats death, and victims of shoot-and-run incidents reappear to be gunned down once again. While the idea of controlling a criminal character seems worrisome, the lack of an emotional link with the character or his or her victims has the effect of reducing the format to mildly cathartic entertainment.

Games makers are interested in the game play, to the point where moral judgments are just another feature of the game engine. Playing the bad guys becomes just a matter of deciding on the black or the white in a game of chess. If the bad guy is an interesting and fun counter in the game, why not play him?

1. **Schwarzenburg** by Radon Labs, the SS commander flawed by his ideology. All of the main characters were sculpted in clay as part of the development process.
2+4. Tanner in action in **Driv3r** by Reflections and adversary Jericho. The level of realism now being achieved by recent games is incredible.

3. Villains from **Starsky and Hutch**, developed by Mind's Eye. Although the movie and TV show are live action, the developers went for a cartoon style, which would work better than realism in the game.

7

INSIDER SECRETS: WORLD DOMINATION

EVIL GENIUS

Ajibayo 'Siku' Akinsiku, Visual Director at Elixir Studios, gives us his thoughts on character design. We have been asked to point out that that these are Siku's views: they do not necessarily express the corporate philosophy of Elixir.

How important are characters to the video game?

'That would depend on one's definition of "character" and "game". Games like *Tetris* or *Space Invaders* are devoid of characters in the traditional sense yet are robust designs and have perpetual game-play value. So, in a sense, a "characterless" game need not be a game of lesser value – one can still inject story-telling features. For example, "One little blue brick fell in love with a pretty pink brick, a big red brick came and took the pretty pink brick away." In this case it no longer matters that these are bricks, it's still a "boy meets girl" story. Once a storytelling element is introduced characters become indispensable.'

In what ways do you think game characters differ from characters in other media, such as movies or literature?

'Characters in games and other media differ in absolutely no way whatever. There are mechanical issues but these issues cut right across the board. A comic-book character will translate differently in movies or literature because each medium's capacity allows for unique traits, but the fundamental principles are universal; fundamentals never change! One should not confuse superficial trait for fundamental rule.'

1–2. Many pieces of artwork are created both for final marketing but also as explorations into the style and feel of the game.
3. Eli the Henchman.
4. The beautiful but deadly Alexis.
5. The mad biochemist.

What would you say are the special requirements of a character?
'The emphasis isn't what makes game characters unique but what makes them similar to every genre. For example, characters that people react to empathically are good characters, the aim therefore would be to emulate that fundamental rule in a given game. I do not consider the limitations or advantages of game-character development as special since every genre has specific requirements. An example would be a low-budget television series of *The Hulk* having greater restrictions than its blockbuster movie counterpart. On the other hand, the television series has a much longer time to tell Hulk's story.

'On the part of games concepts, I approach it exactly the same way I approach comic-book character design or film. Game concepts require more discipline; this would relate to biped restrictions, skinning issues, and design, but on the whole, fundamentally, my approach is the same though one may end up with very different results.'

1. Ivan the Henchman.
2. Top Hat.
3. Henchman.
4. A henchwoman scientist.
5. The beautiful but deadly Alexis.

7

2   3   4   5

What extra qualities make a game character stand out from the crowd?

'Again, there is no special game requirement here. Designing a character that stands out from the crowd simply means deploying solutions rarely seen or unseen in that particular genre. In the case of *Evil Genius*, we exploited Art Deco aesthetics to acquire the *EG* look. That rule would have applied in TV or movie animation. What made the visuals of EG special was the fact that no-one had done it before in games.'

Do you look to expand character IP beyond the games industry?

'That would be an issue for IP owners, however, it is something I debated at comic-book festival panel debates. I insisted that comic-book publishers should have diversified into games long ago – to my mind, game development was an extension of what comics were doing. Entertainment for the young at heart and the young in age. If it's entertainment then, where viable, one should seek to exploit the property in other media.'

Where do you think the game character will be in the future?

'The game character will become a highly consumable product in the future. Both technology and good old-fashioned character development will see to that.'

How do you make decisions about what characters a game is going to have, and what they look like, their personalities, etc.?

'The lead designer generally prescribes the rules, though in a Concept team, a closer, symbiotic relationship is developed. The start of a good concept process is always the brief. The better the brief the better the chances of a successful design. In the absence of a brief (which does not mean absence of game-play design/premise) you create a solid brief yourself. A brief is all about rules that the fictional world places upon you; both mechanical and artistic.'

Currently, what are the sort of technical limitations you have to take into account when designing game characters?

'Genre, market, platform, and resource are just some of the issues that may have an impact of a technical nature on the creative

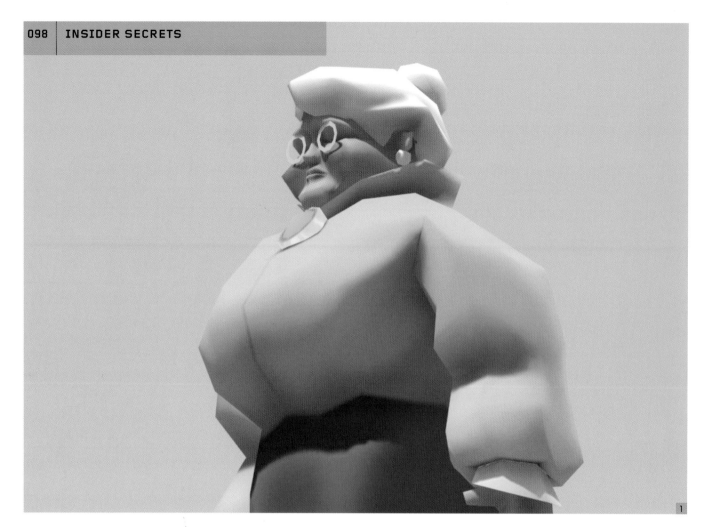

1

process; however, the issue of resource requires, persistently, the greatest attention in this regard.

'I view technical limitations as an opportunity for lateral thinking. In *Evil Genius*, with over 100 unique characters and limited biped and animation options, one very quickly becomes creative. In designing characters for *EG* we decided to utilize six biped dimensions reflected as six body types; Large Male, Average Male, Unique Evil Genius, Unique Freak, Female, Short Generic. These categories would be the basis for our 120-plus characters. We decided early in the concept process that a range of biped variations was crucial to *EG*. We were determined not to rely on texture swaps for variety and thus, over 100 of our characters are geometrically unique. This early resolution created the rules of engagement, every character designed around a specified biped.

'Sometimes we were forced into unknown territory and we came up with astonishing solutions we would never have imagined without the limitations of engine requirements or programmer stipulations. One good example is the Minion Chemical Suit. The perfect spherical headgear was a problem-solving device enabling the transparent glass to constantly revolve. To the viewer it would appear fixed. We would never have thought of a large perfect sphere for a headgear and I previously never thought it would work, not in a million years, till I tried it.'

What impact has the increasing sophistication of game engines had on character design?

'In my opinion, it has had less effect on character design than other aspects of game development. Character design is based on traditional principles. Technology or budget-based limitations are neither here nor there. It's just another environment to apply old principles in ingenious ways.'

How do you work with character design? Is it a specialized area handled by one or a group of artists?

'There are two ways of handling character designs; by the hand of one artist or a team of artists. There are then two ways of stylization; a style based entirely on the sketches of one artist, thus his style directing the visuals, or a style based on agreed criteria.

7

1. The Matron Henchman.
2. Kenya the Saboteur.
3. The Diplomat.

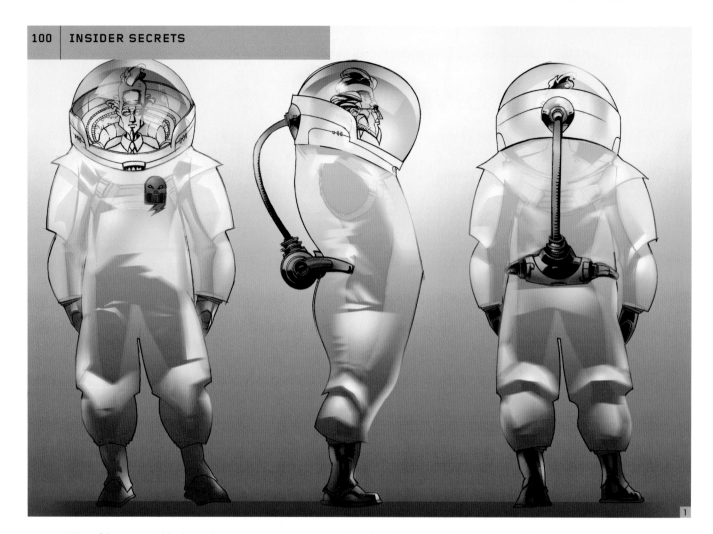

'Either of these are viable depending on resource, requirement, circumstances. At Elixir, we have utilized both methods: a team of artists concepting provides energy and enthusiasm, especially when modellers and texture artists are contributing concepts; on the other hand it makes for incoherence in terms of style. I would recommend "group concepting" for projects with no or low stylization value. However, a highly disciplined group will be able to commit a style to consciousness and replicate that style on demand.'

How important is the back-story to a game character?

'In the absence of one, a concept artist tends to build a sketchy back-story consciously or unconsciously. However I do not rate back-stories highly; I do not see how Mr. X's drugged-up sister impacts on his hair style, but I do see its merits. More of the time I would say the concept art lends itself to suggesting more relevant back-story.'

Visually, what do you think works and doesn't work with characters in the game-space?

'A most common fault in games is the layering of highly detailed textures on low poly-geometric surfaces. Low-polygon surfaces cannot plausibly support highly detailed textures and highly detailed texture tends to expose low-poly structure. It would be far more prudent to layer a less detailed texture over a low-poly object in a low-poly world, that would ensure compatibility and our minds aren't telling us it's wrong.'

1–3. The mad biochemist in concept, with texture maps and as the final model. Notice how the green light from the helmet is painted onto the texture map.

7

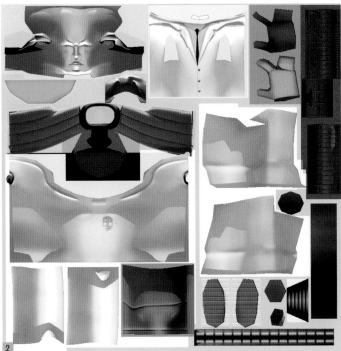

2

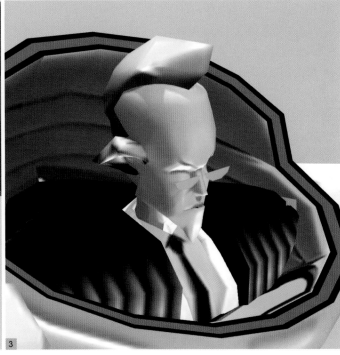

3

Many games strive for realism in style. Would you like to comment?

'Realism is a Western preoccupation, which will gently fizzle out with the advent of mass-market appeal and technology two or three generations away.

'You may find it curious that I imply technology will contribute to the demise of hyperrealism, for the given wisdom is to assume that technology in itself will drive realism to new heights. On the contrary, I suggest that that effect will be short-lived and the reverse will become the norm. The *Final Fantasy* movie is a snapshot of what will happen when we are able to create movie-quality real-time graphics. We will simply switch off when confronted with hyperreal corpses trying to convince us they are human and all the time our unconscious and conscious will scream out, "No you are not!"

'Remember hyperrealism of the seventies in art? Technology accorded us modern equipment, making it easier to achieve. We look back now and squirm just like we do recounting hyperperfect music of the eighties during the dawn of digital music.'

What are the most important elements you are looking to achieve both in character design and animation?

'Emotional content.'

What would you say are the challenges to bringing cartoon characters from a traditionally 2D medium into real-time interactive 3D?

'Winning over an audience bloated on a diet of realism. That audience will not necessarily dictate things when the games industry finally matures and a new generation of "ten-minute" gamers floods the market.'

MAINLY BY CUNNING 8

THE TRICKSTER

'CUNNING SURPASSES STRENGTH.' GERMAN PROVERB

WRAPPING THE SHADOWS AROUND HIM HE CREEPS FORWARDS, EACH FOOT PLACED PRECISELY, EARS SHARP FOR ANY SOUND AND EYES FIXED ON HIS PREY. SO CLOSE HE SMELLS THE PATINA OF SWEAT ON THE BACK OF THE GUARD'S THICK NECK, HE SLIDES THE BLADE IN AND TEARS IT ACROSS, THE ONLY SOUND A SHORT GRUNT, AND BLOOD SPLASHING ON STONE.

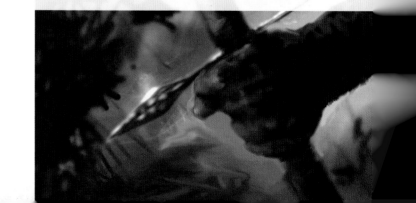

Thief: Deadly Shadows by Eidos and developed by Ion Storm.

Tricksters who have appeared in myth, literature, and movies over the years have proved interesting characters because audiences don't know what to make of them. Even the most famous of all tricksters, James Bond, though compelling, is a difficult man to trust. Whose side is he on – spy, counterspy, double agent? In the final analysis perhaps they are only loyal to themselves.

The trickster, although relatively rare in the video game, is the one character to bring new and extended game play directly from the elements of his type. A trickster thinks like a game player, with a game plan. Whether it's to destabilize a rival country by swamping its markets with cheap grain, tricking a princess into marriage, or simply deciding on which side of a victim's neck to pass a garotte, the trickster is working to a carefully considered strategy.

The *Thief* series by Eidos, and special forces games such as Tom Clancy's *Splinter Cell*, employ trickery in a more directly physical sense, that of stealthy assassination. In *Thief* you play Garret, a freelancer, out to steal what he can from the rich, in a night-shrouded medieval city. Each robbery or assassination involves Garret creeping through the dark, silent and hiding in the shadows to avoid the attentions of the guard. Every step, movement of the knife, even breath, is a strategic move.

The *Commandos* series by Pyro Studios and *Silent Storm* series by Big Ben are examples of character-driven, squad-based strategy games. Both are set in WW II and feature special operations units on dangerous missions behind enemy lines. Naturally, stealth, deception, and cunning are all required, using the varied skills of the team. Both games, although 'zoomed' out for a tactical viewpoint, make full use of the characters – not just their different skill stats, but their personalities, too.

1. **S.T.A.L.K.E.R.: Shadow of Chernobyl** by GSC Game World. In the years following a second explosion at Chernobyl, the curious sneak into the site to investigate reports of weird incidents. It's interesting that the characters have no motive other than thrill-seeking.

Opposite. Rhama, Faith, and Mihoko. **Galleon** by Confounding Factor was devised by Tomb Raider creator, Toby Gard. The characters have a carefully considered style that is unique to the game.

8

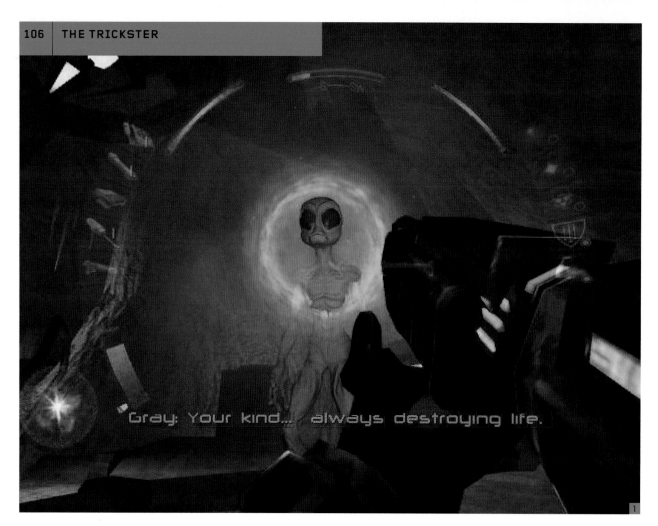

Gray: Your kind... always destroying life.

High-tech espionage is used in Ion Storm's excellent *Deus Ex* series, from the creator of *System Shock* and *Ultima Underground*, Warren Spector. It's set in a near future where anarchy reins and a sinister secret society seeks world domination. Rookie UNATCO agent J.C. Denton receives nanotech and bionic body enhancements and is dispatched on secret missions to bring order to chaos. Denton infiltrates the enemy's bases, assassinates their commanders, and blows up their installations. He has to use caution and guile for the enemy are stronger and numerous.

In its widest interpretation the trickster, as strategist, can be applied to a number of other game characters. Sherlock Holmes and other detective characters are, in a sense, reverse tricksters, where the game is to unravel the trickery of the criminal. Crime detection and the detective are particularly suited to the computer as the game engine is adept at revealing incidents and evidence in timed sequences or as a result of player-character actions.

The cunning character is an interesting waypoint in the videogame because in theory he could be more intelligent than the player playing him. How can that work? In a movie or novel we can enjoy a sparkling, intellectual character without having a brain to match ourselves. Indeed the experience is often stimulating. In games a character's intelligence is represented by a certain array of tools, abilities, or features he or she has at the player's disposal. How the player uses them is limited by his or her intelligence, which by turn sets the upper limit of the character. We will only see characters that dazzle us with their pin-sharp acumen and wit when either the character's AI is better than human, or the game designers invite talented novelists to write the lines.

1. A first-person view showing the neurological enhancements as a head-up display from **Deus Ex: Invisible War** by Ion Strom.

Opposite. **Commandos 3: Destination Berlin.** The Green Beret, Driver, Sniper, Sapper, Thief, and Spy. The characters all have different skills and personalities to bring to the party.

8

INSIDER SECRETS: NIGHT RAIDERS

SILENT STORM AND ETHERLORDS

VICTOR SUKOV IS AN ART DIRECTOR AT RUSSIAN
DEVELOPERS, NIVAL INTERACTIVE.

**What is the difference between the characters in PC games and
those in movies?**
'The development of computer technologies has made game
characters virtually similar to media types based on visualization.
On the other hand, characters in literature are very different. In
books, we grasp a character through his thoughts and attitudes,
while both in movies and in games we have no access to the
character's thoughts and have to judge from his behaviour only.'

What are the specific demands made of a game character?
'A character must be sexy, diligent, hard-working, and willing to
bring you coffee in the morning. Now to be serious, the demands
depend on the specific game. However, one thing remains: the
target audience should understand the character at once.'

**What technical restrictions do you have to take into
consideration?**
'The only thing (except for having about 100 men and women who,
regardless of what I am going to make, say that they know better)
is the degree of visual detail and complexity. Damn, my childhood
has been given up to reading books about us bravely colonizing
Mars in the twenty-first century; it is now the fourth year of this
bright future, but they still continue telling me: "Man, we can't afford
spending 21,000 polygons for your wizard's pet hamster!"
My books must have been the wrong ones. Now if I stop
bemoaning my fate, I must say that the technologies have become
so developed already that the character designer is not limited
by anything but the game designer's needs.'

1–4. Concepts, screenshots, and
character renders from Nival
Interactive's **Etherlords II**.

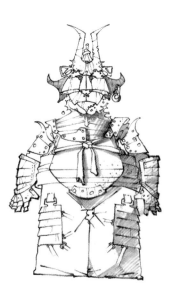

Modelling, texturing, and 3D setup still remain a difficult task demanding high qualification. Do you foresee any changes in the future?

'I don't think that all these difficulties will become more or less serious. To my mind, they will rather proceed to some new level: creating game characters will become very close to creating high-end rendering models, including those for movies. I think this can mean that people new to the gaming industry will become involved in it, such as sculptors."

How do you create characters? Is it a specific field demanding an artist or a team of artists?

'This is how it was in the project on which I am working right now. The game design director told me what the features and special abilities of all the characters in this project are, how the player is to feel about various groups of characters, and so on. I made a large number of sketches combining this freak's needs with my own desires. After that, we locked ourselves up in the office for a week and started abusing each other to ascertain which characters

should be accepted and which not. All that remained after the battle ended was given as reference to the team of concept artists. This was the base for the development of all the game's characters with all their details and features.

'Of course, character design is a specific field, and if I was not working with such a gifted team of artists, who were, in their turn, thinking of nothing but the task given to them, it would have not been possible to keep in mind all the requests concerning the characters' outlook, coming in from all the departments involved in the project, the producers, and the marketing office. In general, any group that wants to create a game and has no person or team of persons working only on character design is doomed to the deep of chaos.'

More concepts, screenshots, and character renders from Nival Interactive's **Silent Storm.**

8

What qualities do you look for in artists and students who want to join the industry and specialize in character projecting?
'First, pliability of thought. Second, richness of mind. Third, freedom from being "looped" on a single style of art. But the main thing is being open to apprehending other people's ideas.'

Is a character's background really important?
'It depends greatly on the specific game as well as on its genre. In *Mario*, for example, I didn't care a damn who this small red man was and why he hated turtles: what kept me before the screen was simply the prodigious game play. But in any production about Spiderman, if you cast aside the story of Peter Parker, what remains – the leaps of a ninny wearing a red-and-blue latex suit – becomes very odd. As both a gamer and a professional, I prefer characters with deep, detailed back-story.

'Generally speaking, I think that the late 1990s have become a moment of transition from – comparing the mass-media consumer to a primitive Cro-Magnon man – worshipping the god of sky and his celestial blazes to asking questions like what lightning is, what is sky made of, and is there a god behind the clouds? It is quite possible that in the nearest future, "amotivational" characters lacking personality and "private life" will answer the needs of the mass market no more.'

How important is the impact of the possibilities of game physics on a character, such as rag dolls, soft textile simulation, etc.?
'It depends greatly on many things, but every complicated interaction of a character with the environment is cool because it makes the character more "real", making the player believe even more, which, I think, is the main task of the character designer.'

IT COULD BE YOU

THE MODERN EVERYMAN

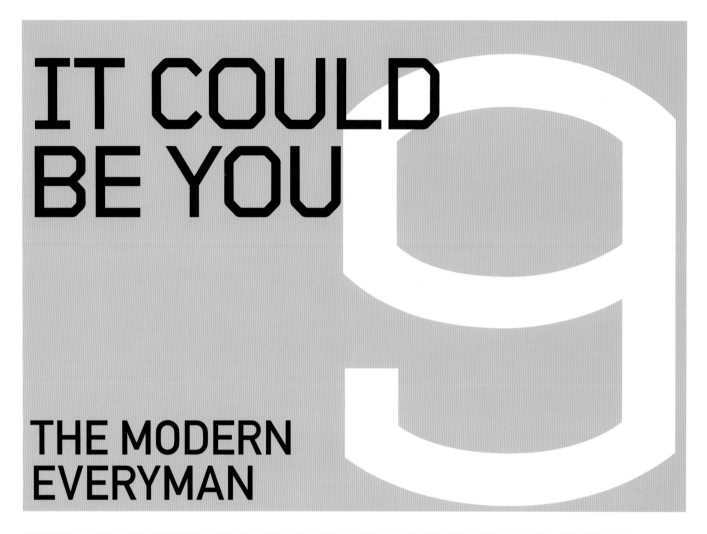

'THIS IS AS TRUE IN EVERYDAY LIFE AS IT IS IN BATTLE: WE ARE GIVEN ONE LIFE AND THE DECISION IS OURS WHETHER TO WAIT FOR CIRCUMSTANCES TO MAKE UP OUR MIND, OR WHETHER TO ACT, AND IN ACTING, TO LIVE.'

GENERAL OMAR BRADLEY

YOU CAN HAVE EVERYTHING YOU WANT — THE PERFECT MARRIAGE, A CLUTCH OF SUCCESSFUL OFFSPRING, A FABULOUS MANSION, A GARAGE FULL OF SUPERCARS, A LUXURY YACHT, ALL THE LATEST GADGETS AND GIZMOS, AND A BANK ACCOUNT BRIMMING WITH MILLIONS. YOU CAN HAVE ALL OF THIS ... WHILE YOUR REAL LIFE DRAINS AWAY.

Space Colony by Firefly.

1

Surely the video game is the ultimate escape from the grind of everyday life? The majority of games are all about escapism yet one game, *The Sims*, saw the potential of the domestic dream. *The Sims* was designed by Will Wright, developed by Maxis, the makers of *Sim City*, and released in 2000 to become the best-selling computer game ever. Its concept, of simulating everyday life, is virtually unique in gaming. Even with the huge success of *The Sims* it's surprising that the industry has been so slow to explore this untapped genre. This is partly because *The Sims* is one of the few titles to appeal to those other than the usual gamer – namely girls and women. The industry, which is predominately male, still has difficulty understanding why *The Sims* was so successful.

In *The Sims* the player creates a family by designing each character's sex, age, clothing, hairstyle, race, and appearance. The player then goes on to adjust a set of personality traits such as playfulness, shyness, seriousness, neatness, and laziness. It is possible to input approximations of these elements based on real friends and family to create virtual versions of them. During the game the player has to micro-manage the family, from getting a job to going to the bathroom, with the goal of improving their lives in love, relationships, and, of course, materially. In *The Sims 1* these were the limits of the character design while *The Sims 2* adds, among other things, aging, personality-trait inheritance, and a more sophisticated AI.

1. **The Urbz** by Maxis takes the Sims to the city.
2+4. Characters in Firefly's excellent **Space Colony** have pre-authored personality traits, which, akin to

Animal Crossing, are credible and appealing, however eccentric some of them are.
3. **The Sims 2** by Maxis.

9

2

3

4

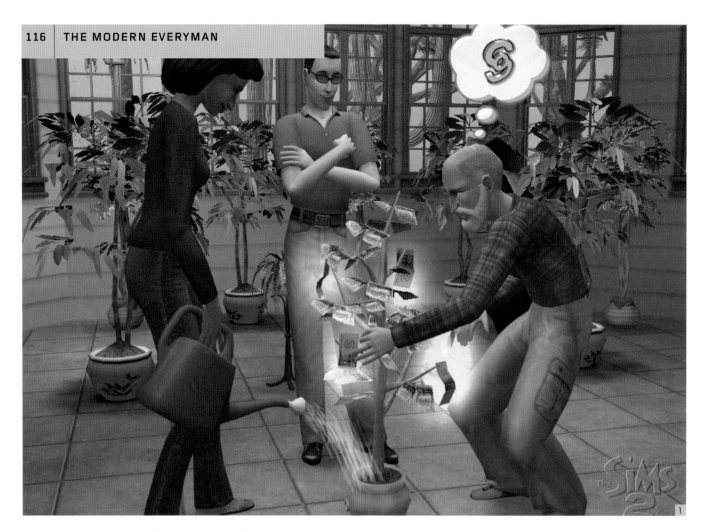

The Sims is an interesting combination of fascinating life-simulation and a management strategy game, not dissimilar in basic play to the Sim City that proceeded it. The core of the idea is character-based, yet the characters behave like soulless automata. This is for a couple of reasons. The first is that characters are designed by the player, which leaves the character with little mystique in terms of their personality, motives, and beliefs, a mystery that in real life preoccupies most of us about our fellow beings. The second is simply down to the technical limitations of current AI systems. A well-designed character, from a novel, movie, game, or whatever, is constructed from a mass of subtle details beyond their basic personality traits. They are moulded by their background, parentage, and experience, all of which is generated by the mind of an author. Interesting characters are unlikely to emerge from AI systems until they become sophisticated enough to process the vast amount of real-life data experienced by the average human being. Even then, do we really want it to generate a realistic proportion of the mundanity common to real life?

Nintendo's Animal Crossing is similar in some respects to The Sims but takes a more directly authored approach. The player directly controls a character with similar goals to The Sims, making money and improving relationships. The difference is that all the other characters with whom the player's character interacts have personalities written and implanted by the game creators. As a result, Animal Crossing is populated with believable characters who are funny, sometimes unpredictable, and very endearing. The player has to try to understand their personalities and discover ways to get along with them. It is, perhaps, a little odd how a game full of cutesy animal characters can be closer to the way human relationships work than any other, however realistic.

1. **The Sims 2** by Maxis.
2. Nintendo's **Animal Crossing.**
3. **Singles: Flirt Up Your Life** by Rotobee is a game where the player character has to seduce the other character into bed, usually by performing a series of tedious domestic chores.
4–5. Every soldier is one of us. Character concepts from **Medal of Honor: Rising Sun** by EA Los Angeles.

HANDS ON: THE ART OF MODELLING

THE 3D WORLD

3D environments have become ubiquitous in games, mainly because of the flexibility they offer, the move towards realism, and massive advances in 3D-display technology. Very few modern games use 2D graphics, and even if they do, the characters are typically created and animated in 3D then rendered into 2D frames. The closest animation style to computer 3D in the real world would be 'claymation' animated puppetry, such as Aardman's *Wallace and Gromit*.

Creating characters for a real-time 3D engine is a complex and demanding task. The models are usually built by a 3D artist in a standard 3D modelling software program such as Discreet's 3D Studio Max or Newtek's Lightwave. The artist begins modelling by placing polygons in the virtual space and linking them to create a mesh. Polygons are three or four points filled with an infinitely thin surface. Once in the game the graphics engine calculates where the mesh of polygons is from the point of view of the player character and generates the image, a single frame, for display on the screen. How fast the game engine generates the frames is dependent on how efficient it is, the complexity of the scene, the chosen screen resolution and the speed of the graphics hardware. To create smooth, flicker-free animation, at least 20 frames have to be generated every second.

The quality of the 3D character has improved a lot over the past few years as hardware speed has increased, allowing far more polygons per character to be processed by the game engine.

1. Although the game world is full scale and realistic, the surface finish on the Transformer models is reminiscent of the scale of the toys from which they derive.

2. Process from sketch to final models. Sarge and Rollarm from **Transformers: Armada,** developed by Melbourne House.

3–5. **Legend of Kay** by Neon studios. Here we see Kay as a wire-frame model, UV mapping, the texture map, and, finally, textured. The chequered image seen in UV editing is used to look for stretching or pinching of the texture.

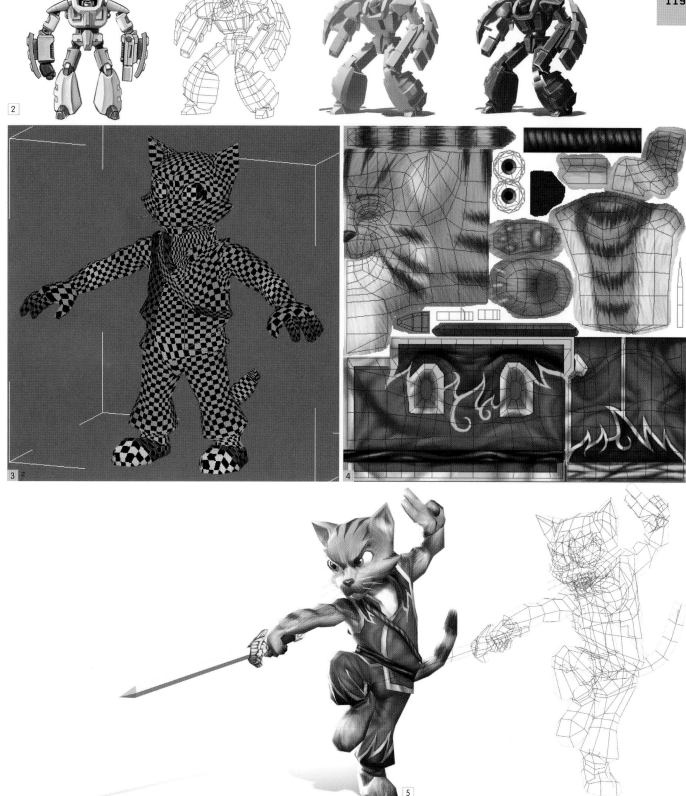

2

3 z

4

5

Moran Gangs character

Characters in games such as *Quake* (1996) were restricted to a few hundred polygons whereas a recent game like *Doom 3* (2004) can process thousands, and the figures keep increasing. While polygon restrictions are becoming less of a concern for 3D artists, being skilled at creating efficient models using the minimum polygons to maximum effect is still important.

THE MODELLING PROCESS
Building an animated game character is split into three distinct but slightly overlapping tasks. The whole process is more or less the same as that used in the 3D animation industry in movies such as Disney's *Toy Story*, except the particular game engine may have special requirements.

POLYGON EDITING
How the artist builds a model varies. Some would begin at the head, for example, building by placing individual points and linking them to make polygons. Others may use primitive shapes supplied with the 3D software, such as spheres and cones, and sculpt them like digital clay into the shapes they require. Sometimes character models, especially humans, can be formed by adjusting commercial pre-built basic models. Generally the artist wants to form larger shapes, such as a thigh, from fewer polygons, while the majority are consumed in detail such as the hands, feet, and face. Special consideration has to be made for the model flexing during animation, so enough polygons have to be placed around the joints, the mouth – if the character speaks – and eyes.

9

In Engine

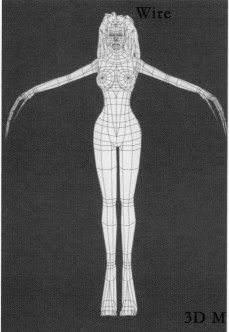

Wire

3D Max

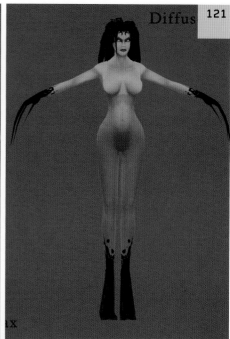

Diffus

TEXTURING

Surface detail and colour on a model is created by wrapping a 2D bitmap painting, called a texture map, around the polygon mesh. Before the character model can be textured, a UV map, which holds the positioning information for the texture map, has to be created. The model has to be cut up and each of its faces unfolded and laid flat; more or less the reverse of tailoring a suit. This 'peeled' version of the character then forms the template to which the texture artist paints using a 2D paint program such as Adobe's Photoshop. Once complete, the UV map is applied and the painting appears in the correct position on the model. Some artists use 3D paint programs, such as Maxon's Bodypaint or Right Hemisphere's Deep Paint, which allow them to paint directly onto a 3D model.

RIGGING

The final process is rigging, which is the creation of a virtual skeleton connected to the mesh to allow the animator to manipulate the model. It mimics all the actions of the human skeleton, such as joint rotation, and may also feature inverse kinematics, an animation tool where the animator can pull on a limb and the rest of the body will follow realistically. Rigging is complex and the final setup requires much testing and adjustment.

1. Spellbound's **Chicago 1930**. An interesting study in the translation from 2D concept to 3D model.
2. Terminal Realities' **Blood Rayne** showing wire frame and textures.

3. We can see the relative density of polygons in different areas of Jade's face. Ubisoft's **Beyond Good and Evil**.

BABY FACE

10

MANGA

THEY CAME FROM THE EAST, FROM THE PAST, PRESENT, FUTURE, AND FANTASY. THEIR EYES BIG, BUT FAR FROM INNOCENT, THESE CHARACTERS, WITH THEIR CHILDLIKE VISAGES AND BLUE SPIKY HAIR, CAN PUNCH AND KICK WITH THE BEST OF THEM. THEY COMMAND GREAT EMPIRES IN THE VIDEO GAME UNIVERSE, DOMINATING WHOLE GENRES WITH THEIR CLEAN-CUT STYLING AND FRANTIC GAME PLAY. MANGA IS NO LONGER THE PRESERVE OF THE EAST BUT A TRULY INTERNATIONAL PHENOMENON.

Ingrid from **Fightin' Jam** by Capcom
Production Studio 2. The sweet, doe-eyed
Manga girl actually turns out to be a super-
tough fighter who's a match for any man.

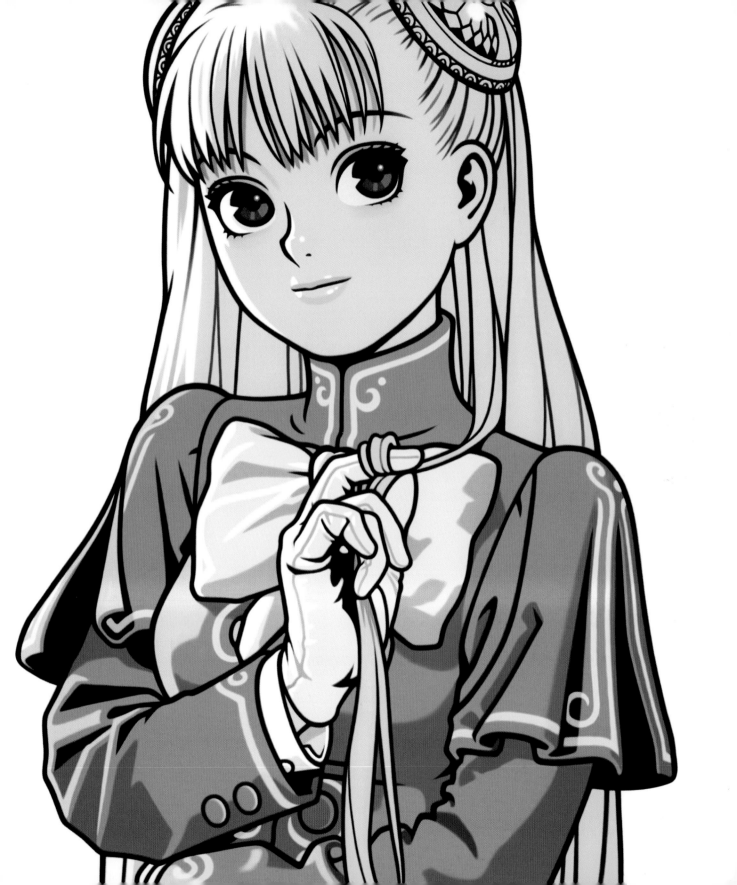

1   2   3

Manga is the Japanese word for comics, though it has become associated with the style of big eyes and a small mouth, a style that has crossed into animation, to become Anime, and the video game. The word was coined in 1815 by the artist Hokusai from 'man', meaning whimsical and 'ga', meaning picture. The Japanese comic-book market is huge, with publications enjoyed by all ages and strata of society, from children through to hardcore adult Hentai. To place Manga as a chapter in its own right is not really correct in this book, which is themed on character types, as it is a style, and as such can encompass any character type. However, the fact that Manga influences virtually all Eastern game design and a proportion of Western game design, too, means it deserves a special place in the annals of game-character art.

The history of Manga stretches back to the sixth and seventh centuries when Buddhist monks drew narrative on scrolls depicting animals behaving like humans. At around the thirteenth century the practice migrated to temple walls where the drawing became more caricatured, establishing the visual style common to Manga today. In the early 1600s the drawing moved to wooden blocks with drawings that were often erotic, an ever-popular theme in the genre. The first books appeared in 1702 when Shumboko Ono, a celebratory Manga artist of his time, strung what had previously been disconnected images into a sequence. It was after World War II that the industry really took off, when small companies produced very cheap comics called 'little red books'. Since then the industry has expanded and branched out to entertain adults and children alike.

The fascinating aspect of Manga is the way in which it works for every player age group whereas Western comic styles, particularly American superhero style, are less comfortable in some genres, such as children's games. Manga is, of course, perfect for children's and cutesy-style games, dominating this end

1. Concept painting from **Onimusha 3** by Capcom Production Studio 2.
2. Subtle Manga character design by Kazuma Kaneko, the artist behind the excellent **Shin Megami Tensei: Nocturne** developed by Altus Software.

3. **Gitaroo Man** from Koei shows how a naive style can work well in video games.
4. **Harvest Moon: A Wonderful Life** by Natsume shows an extreme version of Manga style where toddlers assume adult roles.

5. **Astroboy,** created by artist Osamu Tezuka, is a classic 1950s Manga character and is now in a Playstation game developed by Sonic Team.
6. **Megaman** by Capcom Production Studio 3 is classic Manga.

1

of the market with companies like Nintendo. Children's Manga splits into substyles. There is the cute graphic style found in games like Nintendo's *Animal Crossing*, loosely based on the children's Little Kitty book character, through *Pokémon,* to the comic action style of Bandai's *Dragonball Z*. At the older age range most beat 'em ups are Manga in origin with titles such as Capcom's *Street Fighter* series, *Tekken,* and *Dead or Alive*, famous for its busty females. There are also many adventure and role play titles, such as *Onimusha* and *Crimson Tears*, that mix Manga style with adult themes.

So what makes the Manga style work? For the video game the style transfers well onto the small screen; its big head and eyes make it easy to show facial expression even in distant third-person views. For characters the style helps to endear the audience by appealing to a very basic parental instinct – to care for children.

The big eyes and small mouth of the classic Manga character are essentially juvenile features that have the same effect whether they are applied to a child or middle-aged male character.

Beyond Manga's visual style, it also has a number of other key features. Back-stories are usually extensive and detailed, and characters are well rounded and frequently have more depth than initial stereotypes would suggest. In adventure and role play games there is often a lot of – even excessive – dialogue to wade through, while combat is so fast it is difficult to follow. Perhaps the most interesting feature of the Japanese tradition is its huge variety and endless inventiveness, which can be summed up in the long-running *Final Fantasy* series by Square Enix. The game has developed a rich storyline, interesting characters the player can empathize with, and beautiful, luxuriant imagery.

1. **Skies of Arcadia** by Overworks. Manga meets nineteenth-century style.

2-5. **Dragon Ball Budokai III** by Dimps. Just a handful of the many characters from the game who span the entire age range.

10

HANDS ON:
THE GIFT OF LIFE — ANIMATION

ANIMATION PROCEDURE ON *EVIL GENIUS* BY GRANT SENIOR, LEAD ANIMATOR AT ELIXIR STUDIOS.

'*Evil Genius* was a fun project to animate on. The game style is reasonably realistic with an over-the-top, exaggerated feel in the character's design, which allowed the animation to go beyond normal human boundaries and step into the comic world. Early on in development the game's animation style took on a slightly silly-humour flavour, which the team decided they liked and kept as one of the main *Evil Genius* styles.

'The animation approach for *Evil Genius* was relatively straightforward. There are characters in the world, they have personalities, and they have to move around and interact with it. Although a lot of thought goes into how the characters move and who they are, nothing is really set in stone and things can change, and did, all the way through the development of the game (e.g., for reasons of game play speed, turning animations were dropped and the characters spun on the spot).

In the first stages the basics like walking and running around, carrying objects, sitting down, and basic fighting were dealt with. Although this doesn't sound like a lot, it quite often takes a lot of work between the animators and the programmers getting things to work properly in the game environment. Towards the end of *Evil Genius*'s development quite complex character/object interactions were achieved but at the beginning something as simple as getting a minion to get onto and off a bunk from both sides was an achievement.

'Once the designers had properly thought out their ideas and got to grips with how the game was to play and what they wanted in it, the work got more interesting and busier. A large amount of objects needed to be interacted with, traps needed to catch agents, and agents needed to be interrogated and, if possible, dispatched. How the traps and interrogation worked was mainly left up to the animators' imaginations and anybody else who had a good idea.

'The game has nearly 2,000 character animations.'

10

1. Elixir's **Evil Genius**. Characters with their animation control blocks.
2–3. Before and after. Animation from **Evil Genius**.

4. **Impossible Creatures** by Relic. Body parts for animation are connected to each other in a hierarchy so that if, for example, an upper leg is moved the lower leg will follow it.

5. A motion-capture studio during the making of **Metal Gear Solid** by Konami. Motion capture is sometimes used in games where realistic animation is required. Motion data is captured by special cameras from actors performing key moves.

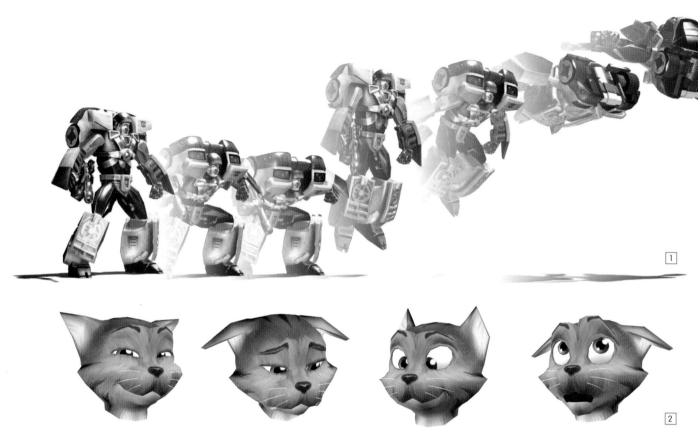

'In the *EG* world there is a huge amount of characters, all of whom need to be animated. The animation is created in the 3D-animation software Character Studio and is then turned into a file that a programmer can use to put in the game to give the characters life. The animator uses the Character Studio biped system, which is basically a set of bones resembling a skeleton to create the animation, such as a walk, or an attack, or a character talking at a bar having a drink, etc.

'In the game there are male and female versions of agents, minions, and henchmen, and they come in five main basic biped sizes. Because all characters in the game can interact with world objects or be caught by all of the traps, this meant a lot of animations had to be created. In most cases this involved reproducing an animation on a female biped, but where possible the character's personality or gender has been included in the animation; for the female characters a more feminine version of the same male animation was created, for the freak a sometimes gentle, docile reaction, the large henchmen a more violent reaction.

'Another area that calls for a large amount of animation variety is combat. Where possible, generic combat moves are used by the lesser characters, like the minions and lower agents, and these were created in a cheesy, brawling fighting style. However all of the henchmen have unique personalities and special abilities, which also required unique animations; the hypnotist has telepathic mind control, the voodoo character uses a puppet to cast spells, Ivan has a rocket launcher concealed in his jacket, etc.

'For an animator, *Evil Genius* was a joy and a challenge to work on.'

1. From robot to road. **Transformers 2** developed by Melbourne House.

2. **Legend of Kay**. Morph targets are different versions of the mesh depicting various expressions. During animation the mesh morphs between chosen targets.

3. A sequence from **Evil Genius**.

10

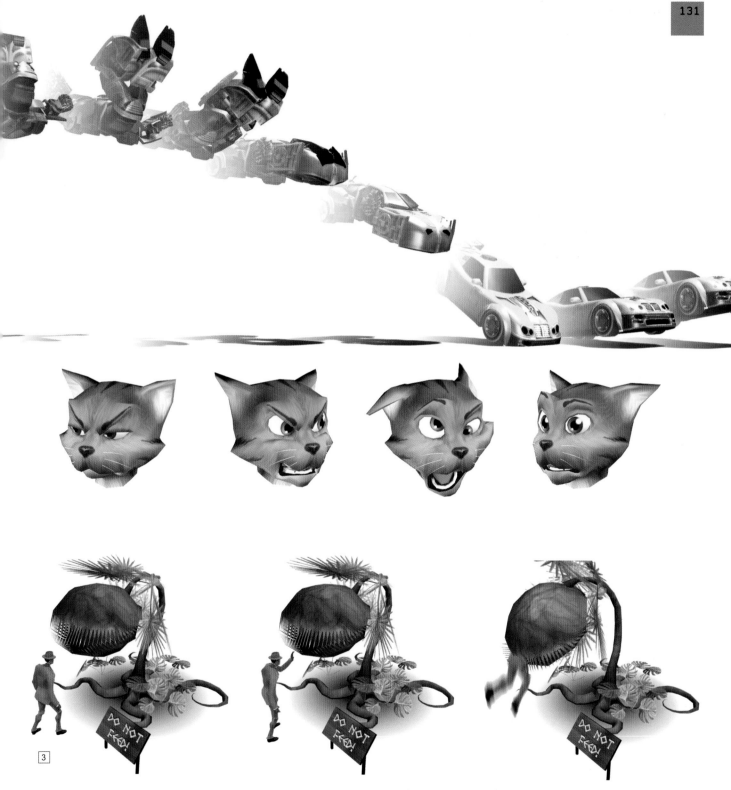

3

BEHIND THE MASK

11

PERSONAE IN FIRST-PERSON GAMES

RUN, AIM, SHOOT. EXPLOSIONS AT YOUR SIDE, BULLETS WHIZZING PAST YOUR HEAD, YOU LET RIP WITH ANOTHER BURST OF AUTOMATIC THEN FUMBLE FOR A GRENADE. YOU ARE THERE, THE CLOSEST YOU CAN GET TO REAL COMBAT WITHOUT GETTING YOUR HEAD BLOWN OFF. THE FIRST-PERSON VIEWPOINT, DEEP IN THE ACTION, IS THE SIGNATURE OF THE MODERN COMPUTER GAME.

Metroid Prime 2: Echoes developed by Retro Studios for Nintendo.

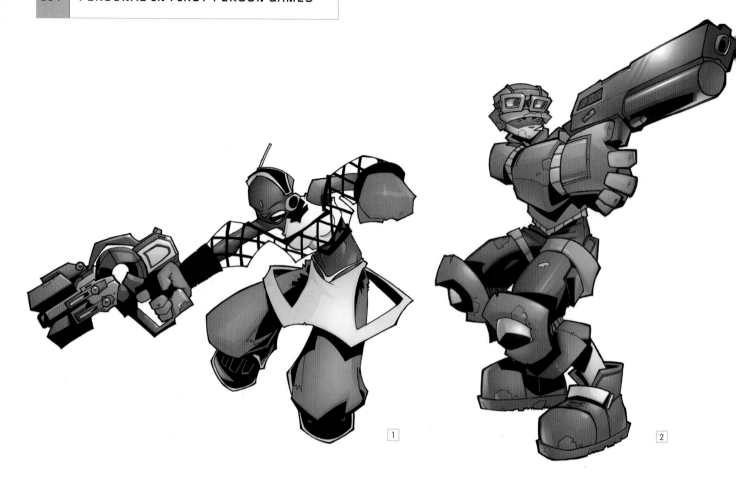

1

2

The idea of looking through your own eyes into the game world, a first-person view, first appeared in 1976 in Atari's *Night Rider*. Prior to this games were always third-person, where the player could see the character object they were controlling on the screen. Other first-person games such as Vectorbeam's *Speed Freak* (1997), Atari's *Battlezone* (1983), and Rainbird's *Starglider* (1986) were all simulations of driving or flying a vehicle. The first game to put the player in the driving seat of a character was FTL Games' *Dungeon Master* (1989), a first-person role-playing game that used simple 2D sprites.

The game that defined the genre of the first-person shooter was ID Software's *Castle Wolfenstein 3D,* published in 1992. Where *Dungeon Master* was first-person it moved at a slow, blocky pace, an incremental improvement on the point-and-click adventures

that preceded it. *Wolfenstein* was revolutionary in that it allowed the player true freedom of movement in a 3D environment. The interaction was more or less instantaneous, making the game character a direct extension of the player. It was a milestone in gaming and in the human/computer interface where the relationship no longer involved a third game entity through which the player had to experience the game. In a sense even the machine itself disappeared as the player stepped into a virtual reality simulation of the game world.

If the player is directly in the game, what happens to the game character? In theory you don't need a character as the player assumes that role, and isn't it the perfect power fantasy to be in the game world, as yourself, mowing down the enemy? However, this isn't the case; all major first-person games have a character

1+2+5. Chastity, Ilsa Nadir, and Viola. Wonderfully exuberant characters from Free Radical Design's **Timesplitters,** a game which breaks from the usual miserable grunge favoured by many FPSs.

3. A proto soldier from **Return to Castle Wolfenstein.**
4. One of **Chrome's** player characters in full battle armour.
6. The chief, the player character from **Halo** by Bungie, never takes his

helmet off even while chatting with other characters during cut-scenes. Was this a deliberate move by the developers to make the character anonymous, allowing players to assume the role more easily?

7. An elite guard from **Return to Castle Wolfenstein** developed by Gray Matter Studios. The series was resurrected in 2001, nine years after ID's original **Wolfenstein 3D.**

3

4

5

6

7

the player controls; even multiplayer death match arenas such as *Unreal Tournament* offer a range of personae to choose from. This third-person character needs to exist to allow players to suspend disbelief and become involved in the game environment, even though during play they see nothing more of their character than a hand wielding a chainsaw.

The real power fantasy being played out is not to be an ordinary human being but instead to revel in an ideal; a muscle-bound hero or curvaceous heroine. Interestingly *Wolfenstein 3D* had a player character, William J. 'B.J.' Blazkowicz, whose portrait appeared on the game dashboard, grunting and suffering with an injury, as a reminder of who you were playing. Perhaps the most persistent of game characters was Duke Nukem, who often uttered his idiosyncratic comments on the situation. Although the game was tongue-in-cheek the Duke exerted a strong presence that bonded player with character. Valve's *Half Life* is a more serious game, with the player stepping into the skin of Gordon Freeman to battle aliens from the planet Xen. When it was released in 1989 it showed

how a considered story and strong central character could engross the player in what hitherto had been a somewhat superficial genre.

Giving the player a character in a first-person game is to give them purpose. The back-story, the reason why you are in the game world hacking up monsters, is a lot easier to explain if there is a character to weave the narrative around, instead of a 'fill your name here' box. Like most entertainment, games are a form of escapism, and if the player plays him or herself they're stuck with one foot trapped in reality.

Where a player character is absolutely required is in the multiplayer environment, because other players need some visual reference to shoot at. However, in arena combat games and online 3D chat rooms, the player character needs to be nothing more than an avatar. The only purpose of these games is to provide a venue for players to either flirt or blow each other up so complex back-stories would be redundant. However, the online reputation and stories of victories do have the potential to create deeper personae beyond the players themselves.

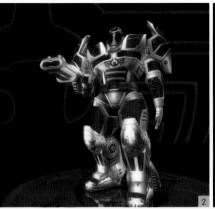

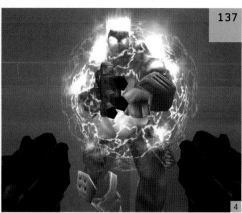

1. A Bond point of view. **Golden Eye: Rogue Agent** developed by EA Los Angeles. It's odd to play such a well-known character without seeing him on screen.

2. **Tribes 2** by Dynamix. First-person shooters are almost a sport.
3. **Doom 3** by ID Software. The original **Doom** set technical precedents, also achieved by this latest iteration.

4. **Red Faction 2** developed by Volition.
5. Logan and Carrie from Techland's shooter, **Chrome.**
6. Hunting for sport. Characters in GSC Game World's **S.T.A.L.K.E.R.: Shadow of Chernobyl** enter the disaster zone.

INSIDER SECRETS: SHIP SHAPE

Richard Albon is the lead character artist at Outerlight. Their first major project, *The Ship*, is a freely downloadable *Half Life* mod, which will expand over time into a high-specification retail product. The game is a character-based murder game where the players are encouraged – by cash rewards from the mysterious Mr. X – to do away with fellow passengers, while being careful not to be caught. Richard describes how he approaches the practical work of bringing some of his characters to life.

MR. X

I am a traditional artist at heart and have designed my characters in the same way for well over a decade. I create the character on paper first, starting with a coloured pencil for the line work. I prefer using coloured pencil (for some reason it has always been orange) as it allows me to be quite free with my movement. When I am happy with the character, I then start to create the finished

line work with an HB pencil, drawing quite heavily so the lines can be read by the scanner. The finished line work is then coloured in Corel Painter. I have always used Painter for my colour work as I prefer the natural media tools.

Mr. X is the almost unseen villain of our project and like all villains he was a lot of fun to create. Seen here in only one of his many costume designs, he is flamboyant, mysterious, and a little bit camp. I wanted to try a different approach for the colouring in this project and built up the tones with layers of diagonal strokes. I wanted to avoid the smooth colour look that can be achieved with computer colouring and tried to give the characters a pencilled look.

Above right. **Concept paintings of Mr. X, Nurse Pat Cleaver, and The Ambassador.**
Above. **Some of the characters as they appear in 3D.**

11

NURSE PAT CLEAVER

A popular character in the office and a personal favourite of mine. A gin-drinking, cigar-smoking bully of a character who was really enjoyable to design and I hope it shows. Each staff member onboard our game environment has a two-tone costume design to create an overall continuity. Again, I owe an awful lot to Painter. Over the years I have found that the fewer tools you use, the better the overall look. I avoid all the custom brushes and special brushes in the program and try to stick to airbrushes and pastels. Each character takes around three days from design to finished colour. There is a staggering number of characters in the game, so I have to be quite quick and often don't have the luxury of bringing them to an ultra-finished quality. That said, each character does have a detailed past created for them and I aim to fit that history into the overall look as best as I can without taking weeks at a time.

THE AMBASSADOR

The Ambassador originates from a fictitious country somewhere in the Balkans. I wanted a regal look to this character, opulent and arrogant with it. As he is an ambassador, I wanted him to be dressed in the clothing of his country, heavy fabrics, and plenty of gold. It took quite a few variations with palettes until I settled with the one you see here. I am extremely happy with the results. The Ambassador was one of the easiest characters to design as I knew what he would look like before I had even put pencil to paper.

DO YOU SPEAK ELVISH?

FANTASTIC CREATURES AND FAERIE FOLK

'ELEN SILA LUMENN OMENTIELVO.' ELVEN GREETING

THE FANTASY LANDSCAPES INSPIRED BY J.R.R. TOLKIEN'S *LORD OF THE RINGS* HAVE LONG BEEN A FAVOURED HAUNT OF THE GAME PLAYER. THE CHARACTERS WHO STEP ONTO THOSE FIELDS DESCEND FROM TWO DIFFERENT GAME GENRES: REGULAR ADVENTURE GAMES AND THE RPG (ROLE-PLAYING GAME). IN THE ADVENTURE GAME THE PLAYER CONTROLS A CHARACTER DESIGNED BY THE GAME MAKER, WHILE RPGS, BY FAR THE MOST COMMON FANTASY GENRE, ALLOW PLAYERS TO DESIGN THEIR OWN CHARACTER.

Naava Daishan from **Kohan II: Kings of War**
by Time Gate. An example of the clean,
American style of 'swords and sorcery'.

RPGs began with the publication of the *Dungeons and Dragons* set of rules in 1974; the seed of a huge new hobby centred around face-to-face storytelling fantasy adventures. Playing an RPG involves the players creating a character on paper, usually from dice rolls, and based on a set of criteria, such as strength, dexterity, charisma, etc. They would then embark on an imagined adventure, the details of which the dungeon master or referee would have prepared in advance. As the character progresses they gain experience whenever they use their skills to good effect, perhaps defeating a horde of goblins or picking a lock. With enough experience they gain improvements in their skills, becoming stronger, brainier, faster, more powerful, and more able to take on tougher challenges. Combined with this is the acquisition of better equipment, magical items, and wealth.

This game system translated easily onto early text-only computers and an offshoot, the MUD (multiuser dungeon), became one of the first multiplayer games. An example of these early games was *Akalabeth* (1979), the forerunner of Sierra's *Ultima* series, which is still successful today. The RPG has changed appearance considerably since those lines of green text on tiny screens. Modern computer graphics have replaced the game world in the player's imagination with fabulous, vast, 3D landscapes, bustling cities, and miles of uncharted dungeon corridor to explore.

1. Concept art in an Art Nouveau style from NC Soft's **Lineage 2: The Chaotic Chronicle.**
2. **Everquest II** by Sony Entertainment Online. The **Everquest** series is one of the longest established MMORPGs.

3–4. Barbarian and comically overweight Ogre from Cyanide Studios' tongue-in-cheek **Chaos League.**

12

2

3

4

Even with the move to the digital realm the basic premise, that of designing and adventuring with your own character, remains the same. The process on the computer usually involves a 'dressing the doll' screen where the player can look at their character and try different elements from fantasy race to hairstyle.

The whole concept of designing your own character is a mixed bag. With traditional face-to-face role-playing games a good player would enjoy 'acting' their character to create a believable personality. Digital worlds tend to be a lot simpler than those run by dungeon masters because machines are unable, currently, to handle the vast variety of possible actions a human is capable of, resulting in rather characterless characters.

Where the RPG is successful is in the creative ownership the player feels for their character, particularly if they have advanced it through several adventures. MMORPGs with their open-ended structure, internal political and financial systems, and, of course, the face-to-face nature of the multiplayer environment, have much greater potential for characters to grow. Already there are player characters in games like Sony Entertainment Online's *Everquest* and Sierra Online's *Ultima*, which have gained mythical status with their own histories of epic adventure. How good these player- and game-system-generated characters are against those created by experienced authors is a comparison yet to be analyzed.

1. Blizzard's **World of Warcraft** is a traditional fantasy world with a slightly humorous edge inherited from the original **Warcraft Strategy** series.

2. Monsters in the field from Arvirago's **The Lord of the Creatures**.
3. Because I'm worth it. Character design by the player from **World of Warcraft** by Blizzard.

12

2
3

HANDS ON: GAME COSTUME

What is a girl to wear when out slaughtering monsters and saving the world? These days it's no good being a plain old polygon seamstress; on today's digital catwalks only the hottest fashion can impress. Designing a character's clothes is as much a part of the process as designing the character itself. What your character wears informs the player about his or her personality, the world in which they live, their wealth, vocation, and game mission.

Designing real-life characters, for example, for a combat simulation such as *Medal of Honor*, requires gathering detailed information about uniforms, correct insignia for the chosen battle group, how the soldiers wore and modified them, and how they'd get dirty and damaged in combat.

FASHION VICTIMS

Fantasy and sci-fi characters require invention, imagination, and a certain flair. A costume has to look good on the character; an apparently simple requirement but with many subtle complexities that a Parisian boutique-owner would be more aware of than the average game artist. For the heroine, vertical stripes help to accentuate the curvier figure, pale alien skin suffers next to yellows, bright hues contrast with dun zombie hordes, and accessories, such as gun holsters, subtly draw attention to the hips. For the hero, big shoulder pads accentuate the masculine shape, power armour should have simple lines, while underpants over tights are definitely outré. Of course, if ever in doubt, you can always rely on black.

1. Ephemera from Terminal Reality's **Blood Rayne**. Detailed sadomasochistic costume design with novel eye socket straps.

Opposite. **Asuka** models the very latest in Japanese game hero chic. **Crimson Tears** by Spike/Dream Factory.

12

1

MAKING A STATEMENT

Aside from the vagaries of vogue, wardrobe design can have an effect on game play. The first is a visual consideration. For many games it is important that the player can easily identify the character on screen, something movie animators have taken into account for years. If characters are wearing clothes that are too close to their backgrounds they risk being lost. The problem can become really acute during battle scenes with multiple opponents, particularly in a third-person view, where it gets so confusing that the player loses his or her character, risking loss of control and frustration. Over-complex designs with excessive colours, pattern, or detail can also risk being lost in the fray as well as jarring on the eye.

Within the game back-story it may be important to use costume to clearly define different teams, tribes, or nations. Apart from the obvious need for identification, differing design will give each faction a cultural background that adds to the game's integrity. Style and standard of dress can also inform the player of social class and wealth which, in an RPG or adventure, could be used as subtle clues to advance the story.

The most direct use of costume is psychological. Different colours, shapes, and textures have a number of associations that effect us both consciously and subconsciously. From a light, floating, flower-patterned dress to hammered-iron armour, everyone has expectations of what a type of character should be wearing. A skintight, shiny bodysuit would be fitting attire for an agile cat burglar while bulky, angular, and metallic armour suggests a strong, heavy, slow incumbent. At a deeper level colour combinations have proven psychological effects. Evil guys are often seen in black or dark red, or a mixture – just think of Dracula's favoured outfit – because red and black are associated with blood and corruption. Yellow and black are warning signs common in nature, while blue and yellow are as optimistic as a sunny morning.

12

2

3

4

5

1. **Middle Earth Online** elf costume design. One of several sketches testing subtle colour variations.
2. Kurenai from **Red Ninja: End of Honor** by Tranji. A low cut is always popular on the game screen, but

there may be practical implications once fighting commences.
3–4. **Skies of Arcadia: Legends** by Overworks.

5. **Fable** by Big Blue Box. RPGs can be demanding on the wardrobe department as the character's appearance should change to match every different item of clothing they can acquire during the game.

NIP AND TUCK

Costume design can have important technical implications for the 3D model, rigging, and animation. The worst offenders are free-flowing textiles, from simple skirts to long, flowing robes. These cause animation headaches, hence the popularity of the skintight catsuit. Ideally robes and trains should be animated as part of the in-game physics engine using soft-body dynamics, a sophisticated system that simulates the real-world behaviour of cloth. While this technology can work it is costly on system resources and currently rarely used. Another option is to animate the flowing cloth using the soft-body dynamics provided in regular 3D-animation programs to generate the necessary frames. The use of bones is best avoided, as it's complicated to set up and fiddly to animate.

The other major problem is polygon intersection. This is where attire overlaps occur, such as big baggy trousers in which each leg can go into the other unrealistically or where a scarf may flap inside the character's body. The best solution is to use a game-physics engine to test for collision and adjust the polygons accordingly. When this isn't practical, careful modelling can usually hide the problem, such as making those trousers less baggy on the inside leg and lightly tacking the scarf to the character's back. These are all very much problems that are currently being addressed by technological advance. In the not-too-distant future it will be possible to model a naked character and his or her virtual wardrobe and, in the same way any real person does, dress them by pulling up trousers and sliding arms into jackets.

Apparel design is as important and wide-ranging an area of a game's art as level design and architecture. Like all entertainment media it borrows from the world around it, but it also has the potential to radiate original and imaginative new styles. Instead of being followers of fashion, games should set the pace.

1. Accessorize. **Ratchet and Clank** by Insomniac Games.

Opposite. **Final Fantasy** on the catwalk. Characters from Square Enix's **Final Fantasy X-2** parade just a handful of outfits from their extensive wardrobe.

MONSTER MASH

13

ROBOTS, DINOSAURS, AND ALIENS

'MEN FEAR DEATH AS CHILDREN FEAR TO GO IN THE DARK; AND AS THAT NATURAL FEAR IN CHILDREN IS INCREASED BY TALES, SO IS THE OTHER.' FRANCIS BACON (1561–1626)

CHILDREN FEAR JUST THE ONE BOGEYMAN. GAMERS FEAR NONE, NOT EVEN THE HORDES OF BOGEYMEN RELENTLESSLY SHUFFLING TOWARD THEM, SNIFFING THE AIR FOR THEIR BLOOD.

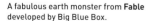

A fabulous earth monster from **Fable**
developed by Big Blue Box.

Throughout history the monster has lurked in the shadows, a manifestation of our fears of the unknown. For early man there were many very real and dangerous monsters created by nature. Wolves, sabre-toothed tigers, snakes, and the mammoth were all creatures to be mindful of outside the comfort of the cave.

Fantastical monsters appear in all cultural myths, from the Minotaur and Hydra of Greek myth through the witches and demons of medieval fairytales to the grey, bug-eyed aliens of today's popular culture. Perhaps the greatest of them all is the dragon, which developed from the discovery of fossilized dinosaur remains, real monsters that once ruled the planet. Indeed nature still has an abundance of hideous monsters scuttling around the

back of the garage or swimming the depths of the oceans, it's just that, thankfully, they are on a manageable scale or miles out to sea.

There are more weird creatures and monsters at large in game worlds now than have ever been seen in movies, literature, or even mythology. The poor things are popular because they make perfect cannon fodder for the trigger-happy player. Monsters can be freely despised as they are unprotected by any legislation against racism, sexism, or indeed, monsterism. It's even acceptable to slice, pulverize, or dice them in a surfeit of gore and avoid the usual censorship afforded to younger players. Interplay's *Carmageddon* (1997) had a gore switch to turn the game's hit-and-run victim's blood green, apparently to tone down the violence.

1. A cast photo of the wonderfully comic set on monsters from Rare's **Grabbed by the Ghoulies.**
2+4. **Metroid Prime 2: Echoes** by Retro Studios. The creatures are imaginative and beautifully conceived.

3+5. Fabulous creature design, Varna and Agni. **SMT: Digital Devil Saga** by Altus.

6. A loper from **Return to Castle Wolfenstein** by Gray Matter Studios. This unfortunate wretch is the result of Nazi experiments. It's interesting that the Nazis and vague terrorists are the only 'real' enemies it is acceptable to hate.

13

3

4

5

6

Where monsters are most appreciated in games is as a creative blank canvas. There are no rules – game artists can explore the limits of their imaginations. Think of the wonderful oily smoke monsters in Sony Entertainment's *ICO*, the eyeball with legs in *Metroid Prime*, and the Intellect Devourer originally from *Dungeons and Dragons* but seen stalking *Neverwinter Nights* (and, I fear, this author!). Unfortunately the imaginations of many game designers are mired in the work of others, particularly Swiss artist H.R. Giger and his *Alien* from Ridley Scott's movie and J.R.R. Tolkien's *Lord of the Rings*, with a dash of John McTiernan's *Predator* here and there. There is no criticism to be made of the source material. Giger's nightmarish vision created a terrifying creature unseen before on Earth, while Tolkien borrowed many of his monsters, goblins, trolls, and others, from existing folktales to recreate them in a fresh mythical amalgam. The problem is that endlessly referring to these masters will only ever produce a pale and degraded imitation instead of thrilling audiences with creations they've never seen before.

1. A demon from Terminal Reality's **Blood Rayne.**
2. Edgar, a really hideous creature from **Midway's Area 51.**

3. **Beyond Good and Evil** by Ubisoft is populated by some wonderfully eccentric creatures.
4. A fabulous Frost Giant from the discontinued **Mythica** by Microsoft Game Studios.

13

From their very first appearance in games, monsters have, on the whole, been on one mission: to eat the player character. Their behaviour is usually less than intelligent and at best bestial, clawing toward their prey as a matter of animal instinct rather than conscious thought. This is both expected and convenient because it requires elementary AI and less strain on system resources. As technology improves, however, monsters are getting a little brighter, by making some attempt to avoid death at the hands of the player. Most games fail to make use of the best trick a monster has up its sleeve, to hide in the shadows, and to prey on our most basic fear – the unknown.

1. Concept art for a truly bizarre monster from Arvirago's **The Lord of the Creatures.**
2. Who could be frightened of these little guys? Whimsical leaf creatures from Nintendo's **The Legend of Zelda: The Wind Waker.**

Opposite. **Dragon Ball Z: Budokai III** by Dimps.

13

INSIDER SECRETS: ODD GLOB

GISH

Edmund McMillan is the artist at Chronic Logic, a three-man independent developer. Gish, the player character of the game, is a weird black blob that behaves like something between oil and molasses. *Gish* shows that it doesn't take huge teams and millions of pounds to create an original and fun game character.

How did you come up with the idea?

'I was up late one night developing characters for another game I was working on at the time and I came up with this little yellow-eyed black demon. As I developed the character he basically devolved into a blob and Gish was born. The next night I came up with the game's basic idea and pitched it to the team the next day.'

What's your thinking while working on a character?

'My main focus when working on a character is usually trying to make it as weird, gross, cute, and unique as I can. I want people to not only smile when they see my work, but question why, and maybe even feel a little dirty afterwards.'

How do you find the experience of working as an independent?

'The beauty of working as an independent for me is the freedom I have when it comes to my design. If I was working at EA and told them that I was going to add a team of faeces-filled sacks with an anus on their heads called the Honey Bucket Boys to a game they were publishing, I doubt I'd be working there after that.'

How big is your team? How long did *Gish* take to produce?

'Chronic Logic is a team of three. Alex Austin did all the programming, I did all the art, and Josiah helped with gathering resources-level design and marketing. *Gish* took about six months for us to finish.'

What do you think of character design and the industry?

'I think most game-character design is very solid. Nintendo's design, especially the cast of characters in games like *Zelda*, *Mario*, *Pokémon*, *Pikmin*, and *Metroid Prime*, is always the best of the best. I am getting a little tired of the more realistic war/mech-looking games these days. They all look the same to me.'

Page 161

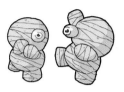

Genus: Obby
Species: Mortobby

Genus: Obby
Species: Zombobby

Genus: Mucilag
Species: Honey Bucket

Genus: Mucilag
Species: Dingle

Genus: Gormander
Species: Coddle Sack

Genus: Begotten
Species: Sapros

Genus: Begotten
Species: Gurge Baby

Genus: Begotten
Species: Paunchy Chops

Genus: Gormander
Species: Nibble Grip

Genus: Zipperhead
Species: Gimper Scamp

Genus: Zipperhead
Species: Ptera Scamp

Genus: Zipperhead
Species: Visceren

Genus: Peashy
Species: Incubus

Genus: Gormander
Species: Tetnis Grip

Genus: unknown
Species: Basenjinn

Genus: unknown
Species: Anujinn

Genus: Gormander
Species: Marrow Grip

Genus: Obby
Species: Scarcobby

Genus: Skinling
Species: bloatling

Genus: Skinling
Species: Weltling

Genus: Skinling
Species: Dumpling

Genus: Peashy
Species: Cereus

Genus: Obby
Species: Bishobby

Genus: Zipperhead
Species: Alter Scamp

Genus: Zipperhead
Species: Sister Vis

Genus: Mucilag
Species: Clot Gobbler

Genus: Mucilag
Name: Gish

Genus: Unknown
Name: Brea

ODDBALLS

14

THE WACKIEST CHARACTERS OF ALL

SO, WHAT'S NORMAL? OUR SENSES, INPUT SYSTEMS, ARE FAIRLY STRAIGHTFORWARD; PICTURES, NOISE, SMELLS, AND TOUCH ARE ALL ROOTED INTO OUR BRAINS. AND THAT'S WHERE THE TROUBLE STARTS.

THERE WAS AN OLD MAN WITH A BEARD,

WHO SAID, 'IT IS JUST AS I FEARED!

TWO OWLS AND A HEN, FOUR LARKS AND A WREN,

HAVE ALL BUILT THEIR NESTS IN MY BEARD!'

EDWARD LEAR

Character renders from Tim Schafer's brainchild **Psychonauts**, developed by Double Fine Productions. The game is original, refreshing, and completely zany, both in its conception and graphic style.

The brain is a huge repository of images, memories, ideas, fears, contradictions, and a million other things, all swirling around just under the surface we call normality. The strange connections and inventions of the subconscious are glimpsed at in dreams, flooding the insane, sought after by artists, and often understood by children. When our normal world is touched by it, perhaps through the work of an artist or waking with the remnants of a dream, we find it both amusing and disturbing. This is the paradox of madness, where we can laugh at crazy behaviour, but fear it in ourselves.

A tiptoe through history in search of the masters of the odd finds them thick on the ground in Victorian England. Edward Lear produced wonderful nonsense limericks and verses, which are humorous and an example of an imagination free of mundane reality. He made all kinds of impossible connections, illustrated with a clear, sketchy simplicity. Today we see his delightful whimsy resonating in game characters such as those found in Nintendo's *Pikmin* and Beep Industries' *Voodoo Vince*.

What Lewis Carroll's *Alice's Adventures in Wonderland* shows is that however mad the world, the practicalities of building it requires sane concentration. The *Wonderland* books sustain a cohesion of ideas throughout, even though the collection of elements, the characters, their motives, and storylines, appear almost arbitrary. The more unfamiliar a world is to the reader, the more the delivery and the explanation of the world has to be clear and well executed or the audience will become lost and confused.

1. Rayman.
2+3. **Gregory Horror Show: Soul Collector** by Capcom Production Studio 3.
4+5. Concept drawings and character render from **Psychonauts**, developed by Double Fine Productions.

6. Berto from **American McGee Presents Scrapland** by MercurySteam. A fabulously inventive set of oddball robots.
7. **Voodoo Vince** from Beep Industries shows how the most bizarre character can make a great game hero.

14

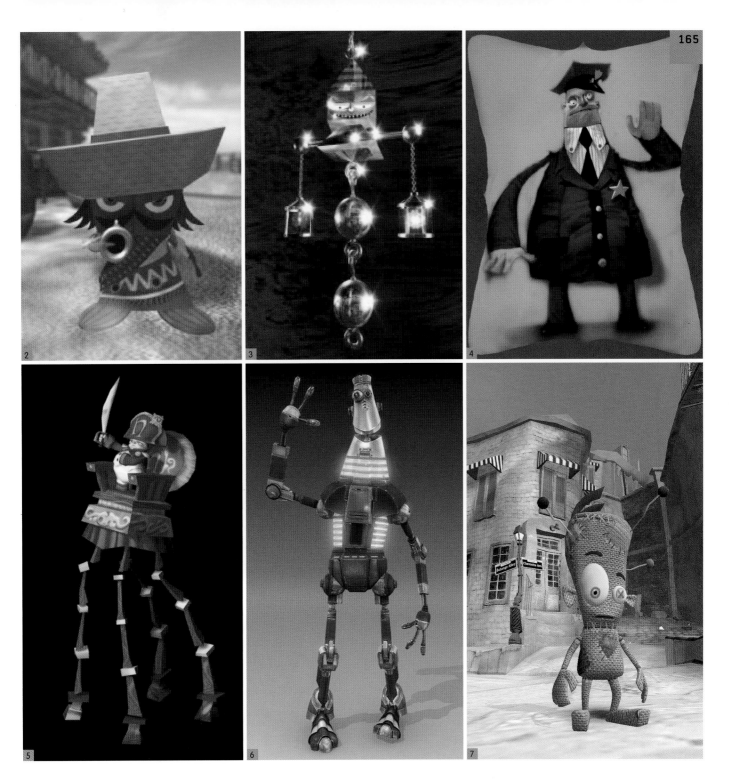

1

2

The same is important for characters who can be madcap; they should be madcap within the limits of their character, otherwise their personalities become too fuzzy for the audience to care about. The importance of all this is magnified in game development where the product's creation is complex and highly technical. Keeping a wacky idea fresh through the long drawn-out process of 3D-model building, rigging, animation, and programming is difficult.

The great joy of the oddball is that bizarre, ugly, or just strange characters can become game celebrities enjoying a lengthy career. Think of *Oddworld*'s Abe, an unprepossessing,

glum character who mopes along on his quest, yet he has a huge following. The same is true of the lanky Crash Bandicoot with his inane grin and bandy-legged run. Playing wacky characters is tremendous fun because they appeal to the freedom of expression we all tried getting away with when we were too young to know better. They typically have a rough-and-tumble style of animation and game play, throwing themselves at the enemy or off cliffs oblivious to injury. Wacky works because it is always entertaining to experience the overflowing imagination of the highly creative as an antidote to the dull conformity of everyday life.

1. A fabulous metal monster from Lucas Arts' oddball shooter, **Armed and Dangerous**.

2+3. Clank character and other concept sketches from **Ratchet and Clank** by Insomniac games.

14

1. Bizarre characters from Beep
Industries' **Voodoo Vince**.
2. Vince in action.
Opposite. **Ratchet and Clank** from
the game of the same name by
Insomniac games.

14

INSIDER SECRETS: INTO THE MACHINE

EYETOY

Masami Kochi, originally from Japan, is lead artist on *EyeToy: Play* from London Studio, published in July 2003 by Sony Computer Entertainment Europe.

What other media did you look at and gain influence from when coming up with the look of these characters?
'Being brought up in Japan, I draw a lot of influence from Japanese media, such as films and television programmes. I am also very interested in fashion, so when I see a cool fashion magazine or advert, I try to dress my characters in similar clothes.'

What kind of audience were you appealing to with the look and feel of these characters?
'I tried to appeal to teenagers, but it's quite difficult for me as European teenagers are more mature than Japanese ones! For instance, as well as teenagers, it's common for Japanese businessmen to read comics on the subway!'

Do you think your Japanese background and training has influenced your style?
'Yes, it has a lot. Some of my art college friends are now actively involved in the TV, fashion, and games industries in Japan, which gives me a great stimulus to succeed!'

Which of the characters is your favourite and why?
'My favourite characters are QT and Oracle. QT because she is clever, sexy, and cool. I wanted her to be a fashion-leader type, and all the boys to fancy her. It took me a long time to create Oracle, because although he is old, I still wanted him to fit in with the other younger characters. After trying many different designs, I gave him a unique head shape for his extra brains, and a monkey as well. He hates wearing old people's clothes.'

Eyetoy's physical interactive game play very much lends itself to stylized, bright, comic characters.

14

When you are designing these characters do you start with their look or with their personality? (Some of them have very noticeable accents and styles.)

'When I create characters, I think about their look and personality together. For example Dex is a lad, so he's crazy about soccer, skateboarding. He has spiky hair, wears a streetwise top, a pair of brand jeans, and funky sneakers.'

How do you work differently when creating a bad guy as opposed to a hero?

'When I start designing, I try to make my bad guys have very cheeky, naughty, and tough personalities, whereas the heroes have to be cool and good-looking. I created the bad guys mostly for 'kung foo' (except for ROBO-BRO who was created for 'boxing-chump'). They are good at martial arts, so they have an oriental flavour, such as the Samurai, Ninja, Noodle Ball, and Chinese Panda.'

BOSSES FROM HELL

15

OBEYING ORDERS

'THERE IS ONLY ONE LORD OF THE RING, ONLY ONE WHO CAN BEND IT TO HIS WILL. AND HE DOES NOT SHARE POWER.' *THE LORD OF THE RINGS*, J.R.R. TOLKIEN

THE BODIES OF THE HUNDREDS YOU HAVE SLAUGHTERED MARK YOUR TRAIL TO THE FINAL CHALLENGE. FEAR CURLS AROUND YOUR HEART, THE CONTROLLER IS SLIPPERY IN YOUR CLAMMY HANDS, THE EDGE OF THE SEAT DIGS INTO YOUR BACKSIDE, WHILE YOUR EYES STARE INCHES FROM THE FLICKERING SCREEN. ARE YOU READY?

Sudeki by Climax.

The game boss is an important part of the formalized structure of many computer game genres, particularly shooters. The first boss appeared in a game called *DND*, an early dungeon crawl created by Gary Wisenhunt and Ray Wood in 1974 on the Plato computer system in Urbana, Illinois. If players survived the entire game they found themselves up against the Golden Dragon, the toughest opponent in the game. The idea was to make the game closer to a story with a beginning, middle, and end. Knowing that an almost indestructible foe lurked in the final stage created a buildup of dramatic tension to the final denouement. As games became larger, less powerful mini-bosses were found denoting the end of each level.

Early side- or vertical-scrolling shooters, such as Nintendo's *E-Type* (1987) with its Dobkeratops (or Doppelganger), set the game play for the boss. Essentially bosses have to be big, so big in fact that they fill the screen, even several screens, so that the player has to scroll down their length – such as the Great Thing in Taito's *Darius* series. In occupying most of the screen bosses could look visually fabulous and terrifyingly massive compared to the player character.

Their size also had an interesting effect on game play in that the player was left with hardly any room to manoeuvre around the screen and was constantly in fear of being crushed, like being stuck in a bathroom with a rampaging rhinoceros.

In most games players have ample warning that they are about to come face to face with their Nemesis. After slaying swathes of the boss's elite guards, the scene ahead will be suspiciously quiet as the player stumbles into the antechamber, a room replete with powerups and equipment. The player, light-headed from the shopping extravaganza, will pick up the last item, the trigger for the grand appearance, and the beginning of the end.

1. **BC** by Intrepid.
2. Strategy titles are one of the few genres to have a final boss as a character yet Elixir's **Evil Genius** and Bullfrog's **Dungeon Keeper** turn the entire game paradigm on its head by making the player the boss. Here is Maximillian from **Evil Genius.**

3. A dragon, the ultimate boss, seen here as a concept painting from **Neverwinter Nights 2**, developed by Obsidian Entertainment (**Neverwinter Nights 1** was developed by Bioware) and reminiscent of the first game boss, Golden Dragon, from **DND.**

5

Typically, if tackled head-on, bosses are impossible to kill; they not only have seemingly impenetrable hides but even if a lucky shot gets through it is little more than a pinprick in its heap of hit points. All the time it rains down blows from a variety of weapons, fists, or flailing tentacles. The boss, however, will usually have a weaker spot, but only a little weaker, because it will still require sustained firepower to breach. There will also be blind spots where the player can stand and fire from or hastily replenish overheated weapons, or sometimes a carefully choreographed pattern of sidesteps is required to avoid the incoming torrent.

In some senses the boss is the heart of most game genres because it provides a clearly defined motive for the player character. As games become more sophisticated it is important for the boss to have a more complex, rounded character beyond being just big and scary. In many game back-stories the boss is the mastermind of whatever evil the player is pitted against and as such deserves a deeper personality. In *Prince of Persia: Warrior Within* bosses such as the Dahaka and Shahdee are deeply integrated into the story, and turn up several times in advance of the denouement to allow the player to get to know them. They are also not tied to a particular place on the level, so can turn and pursue the escaping Prince.

The boss is the ultimate excuse for visual excess. Indeed, the player expects to be impressed by a spectacle, a finale. After all, the boss is the final prize of the game.

The player may be jubilant as he blasts away the boss, but sad too, for when he slumps to the ground it is the final Game Over.

1. **Legend of Kay** by Neon Studios. Poor Kay looks hopelessly small against this mighty boss.

2. Concept drawing of a Witch King from **Lord of the Rings: The War of the Ring** developed by Liquid Entertainment. Break down many classic stories in literature and the movies and it's easy enough to classify the bosses and mini-bosses.

3. Of course, off-screen, game heroes and bosses are often the best of friends. Rare's **Kameo: Elements of Power.**
4. Designing bosses is any creative's dream because anything goes. A wonderful robotic Mergatroid Boss from **Sudeki** by Climax.

15

2

3

4

A GREAT LINEAGE: SQUARE ENIX

The Enix Corporation released *Dragon Quest* in May 1986 while the separate company of Square Co. Ltd. released the first *Final Fantasy* game in December 1987. And so a great games lineage began. Both licences have enjoyed many releases on different platforms over the years. Famously, Square Co. Ltd. released the first CG movie to make use of realistic digital actors, *Final Fantasy: the Spirits Within* in 2001. The companies merged in 2003 to form Square Enix Co. Ltd and continue a remarkable gaming family.

The *Final Fantasy* RPG series is certainly the most famous of Square's games. Over its 12 editions it has built a reputation for engrossing storylines and believable characters. Such is the depth of integration of characters and story that the player will find themselves really emotionally involved; a rare thing in most games.

Visually the series has set a benchmark in the quality and detail of its artwork, in particular the amazing costume of the characters. Their dress has a variety and design style all of its own, drawing on and mixing influences from diverse cultural styles. Even with this eclecticism and detailed adornment each character's general temperament is reflected in his or her outfits. In the later games the characters change their costumes during play, something which is not common in games to any great extent because of the increased cost of assets. This attention to design detail in game play, character, graphics, and story, is evident in every product from Square Enix and has raised them to a position in the industry often envied by other developers.

15

All images: **Final Fantasy X-2.**

15

1. **Unlimited Saga.**
2. **Final Fantasy X-2.**
3. **Star Ocean: Till the End of Time.**

INSIDER SECRETS: WIDESCREEN

ADVENT RISING

Donald Mustard has come from a strong illustration and movie background to create GlyphX Games with his brother, Geremy, as an offshoot of their highly regarded commercial graphics and illustration company, GlyphX Inc. *Advent Rising* is the first title to be released from their epic science-fiction adventure trilogy.

Do you look to expand character IP beyond the games industry?
'Yes, certainly. Generally I see it happening because other industries have seen the massive size of the games industry and its new cultural importance. As games mature you will see a much greater cross-fertilization between the different entertainment media. It's happening now with movies such as *Lord of the Rings*. The movie-makers considered the tie-in games right from the start.

'You will see far more characters crossing from games into other media as character and story development become more important in games. In fact I see the movie and game-industry kind of merging in that movies will become filmed stories from the game and the games become movies you can step into as a player. Pretty much like *Advent Rising*.'

What would you say are the special requirements of game characters compared to other media, such as movies?
'There are several things game characters have to do that are unique to the medium. Some are based on the nature of interaction, for example, how a character reacts to player choices. Others are to do with old-fashioned game play. Characters have to be ready for proportionally far more action than you would get in the average action movie, and able to sustain it over extended periods convincingly. In *Advent Rising* the characters have a lot of cool moves and different actions along with special abilities gained during play, such as psionic powers.

'Then there are the technical differences. A huge part of a movie rests on the work of the actors who really bring the

1–2. Protagonist Gideon Wyeth commands special powers including levitation, shock blasts, and the ability to slow down time.
3. Scene from **Advent Rising**.

characters to life. They deliver the dialogue with a whole range of expressions and subtext. And, of course, there's the "aura" that stars project. I would say that computer games are more akin to the animated movie in that much of the expression is created by the relationship between animation and voice-over artists working closely together.'

How important is the idea of a player character having an active identity of their own in the game, compared with an 'empty shell' a player steps into?

'In coming to the game from a movie perspective we wanted characters that the audience could really believe in. Thinking of, say, Luke Skywalker or Neo from *The Matrix*, they're characters that have their own agenda, their own way of doing things. Although the player interacts with the main character, Gideon Wyeth, Gideon is also very much a character in his own right.

'We also wanted the interaction between the main characters to work at an emotional level that also involves the player, something movies and novels achieve all the time.

For example, you could be playing Gideon to find him falling in love with one of the women while you yourself are falling for one of the other women characters. We want that kind of intensity for both relationships in the game and with the player's involvement.'

In terms of design, what were you looking to achieve?

'We wanted a look that would stand out among other science-fiction titles. Many games have gone for the dirty grunge style that was pioneered in *Aliens*. We were looking for a clean vision of the future, not just in the design styling of spaceships and uniforms, but right across the board. Even the explosions look sharp and clean. The aliens, of course, are very different to the humans; they have a clean white skin, something that is unusual and unexpected in monster design.

1. A turnaround of a Seeker alien.
2. Concept drawings that show the phenomenal level of detail in modern games multiplied across different costumes.

15

'Beyond the styling of the sets and characters we wanted the game to have a cinematic feel. To this end we have used virtual cameras with widescreen movie lenses and throughout the game we have used classic cinematic compositions. We were also looking for a big movie scale with really wide views of epic landscapes, huge starships flying past, and some awesomely big aliens. In *Advent Rising* the player really feels they are in a big-budget blockbuster science-fiction movie.'

To what extent was Orson Scott Card involved in the making of the game?
'Right from the outset we wanted to bring in the help of a professional writer and we were thrilled to have such a prestigious author as Card on board. As a professional he brought a huge amount of new ideas to the back-story and character development. Perhaps the biggest contribution was in creating much of the character dialogue and in directing the voice-over recordings. Games rarely involve professionals from other disciplines even though guys like Card are masters of storytelling.'

Why did you announce *Advent Rising* as a trilogy?
'Well, apart from keeping us in work for a while, we felt that we had a far larger and deeper story to tell than would fit in your average game title. A trilogy also allows more time for storytelling and therefore more time for the player to become involved in the characters. Incidentally, each section of the trilogy will be properly integrated into the other parts. We didn't want the story and the franchise to be diluted by a series of tacked-on sequels. In the *Advent Rising* trilogy you will begin threads of the story that are picked up through the series. In fact, some will only click into place right at the end of the third instalment.'

1–3. Stills from the cut-scene animation sequences that link the gaming sections. They use the game's real-time engine because its quality now matches pre-rendered footage typically used in games in the late 1990s.

15

2

3

INDEX

2D graphics

A method of displaying game graphics using 2D (flat) graphics, but now usually superseded by 3D graphics. Sometimes the games appeared to be 3D but were in fact using 2D images.

3D graphics

The game environment is processed by the computer as a virtual 3-dimensional space. The player's viewpoint in the world is through a virtual camera.

Adventure game

Games that involve interacting with a story.

Arcade game

Games that are played on coin-operated machines in arcades. They also refer to a style of game play, which is usually action-based and simple.

Animation Rig, Rigging

A set of controls used to manipulate a character model during animation. The controls usually consist of a virtual skeleton with 'bones' and joints that mimic the behaviour of a real skeleton.

Beat 'em up

A game genre derived from boxing and other physical contact sports.

Cel Shading

A type of 3D rendering that gives the image a stylized, cartoon-like appearance, as seen in games such as Smilebit's *Jet Set Radio Future.*

CGI (Computer Generated Imagery)

While this can refer to any computer-generated image, it usually refers to pre-rendered 3D stills or animation sequences such as cut-scenes.

Engine

A computer program that performs a set of routine tasks. For example, a physics engine models the mass, velocity, and other physical attributes of objects, while a graphics engine renders images to the screen. These engines are sometimes collected under the term game engine.

First-person shooter

A popular form of 3D action game, typified by titles such as *Doom*, *Halo*, and *Unreal*, where the player fights through complex 3D levels from a first-person point of view.

MMORPG (Massively Multiplayer Online Role-Playing Game)

An online role-playing game environment where hundreds, even thousands, of players assume character roles, usually in medieval-fantasy or science-fiction worlds.

Mod

Some game developers release their game-development editors and toolsets so that players can use their game engine to modify the game.

Model

A 3D object made from a collection of polygons.

Morphing

A method of animation by distorting a polygon mesh. Often used for facial animation where different facial expressions are created called morph targets and during animation the mesh morphs between them.

Platform game

One of the oldest game formats, the player controls a character who has to leap around a vertical and dangerous environment in pursuit of certain objectives. Originally 2D, the platform game moved to 3D with the launch of Nintendo's *Super Mario 64* and Core's original *Tomb Raider.*

Prerendered

CGI images or animations that are calculated from 3D data and stored as complete frames or animations ready for use in a cut-scene or movie.

Polygons

3D objects or models usually consist of hundreds or thousands of filled triangles (or sometimes 4-sided shapes) joined together into a 3D model.

Real-time

Graphics that are rendered as required, as opposed to being prerendered. In-game graphics are usually real-time, as they need to change rapidly to reflect the actions of the player.

RPG (Role-Playing Game)

A type of game that takes its name from the old Dungeons and Dragons style of tabletop game.

Texture map

In 3D graphics, a bitmap image that is wrapped around a 3D model to give it the appearance of having a material or texture, or to add surface detail.

UV map

Shows coordinates of where a 2D texture map is placed on a 3D object.

Wireframe

A view of a 3D model that shows the polygons in outline. Also described as a 'mesh'.

We would like to thank everyone from the games industry who has been so generous with their help including:

Adrian Arnese *Empire Interactive*
Anthony Flack *Squashy Software*
Antony Christoulakis *Neon Studios*
Bernd Beyreuther *Radon Labs*
Brian Woodhouse *Bizarre Creations*
Charles Cecil and Steve Gallagher *Revolution*
Chris Bateman *International Hobo Ltd*
Clayton Kauzlaric *Beep Industries*
Darren Thompson *Firefly Studios ltd*
Dave Morris, Sandy Spangler, Ajibayo Akinsiku (Siku), Poppy Reeve-Tucker and Peter Gilbert *Elixir Studios*
David Swofford *NC Soft*
Dawn Beasley *Climax Group*
Demelza Fryer-Saxby and Nichola Martinus *Microsoft*
Dmitry Kolpakov *Nival Interactive*
Donald Mustard *GlyphX*
Edmund McMillan and Josiah Pisciotta *Chronic Logic*
Farzad Varahramyan, Meelad Sadat, and Alex Armour *Sammy Studios*
Gabor Feher *Digital Reality*
Gail Salamanca *Altus U.S.A.*
Gilles Benois *Eden Studios*
Hanna Gehrke-Rosiecka *Techland*
Helen Myers *THQ UK*

Íñigo Vinós *Pyro Studios*
Jason Fitzgerald *Sony Computer Entertainment Europe*
John Johnson *Relic*
Jon Beltran de Heredia and Raúl Herrero *Arvirago*
Kevin Sheller, Tim Shymkus, Eric Nofsinger, and Josh VanVeld *High Voltage Software*
Laura Heeb *HighWater Group*
Lidia Stojanovic and Jan Sanghera *Ubisoft*
Line Bundgaard *I.O. Interactive*
Lisa Pearce and George Wang *Blizzard Entertainment*
Marc Holmes, Mike Sheidow, and Jason Wonacott *Turbine Games*
Martin Mckenna
Neena Patel and Kevin Leathers *Digital Jesters*
Neena Patel, Richard Williams, and Greg Jones *THQ*
Oleg Yavorsky *GSC Game World*
Pete Hines and Diana Calilhanna *Bethsoft*
Richard Albon *Outerlight*
Simon Callaghan *Atari*
Stephanie Journau *Square Enix Europe*
Todd Sheridan *GlyphX*

Picture Acknowledgments
All games and images are copyright of the original developers and publishers and no challenge is intended to trademarks.